BOYS, BOMBS
and
BRUSSELS
SPROUTS

BOYS, BOMBS
and
BRUSSELS
SPROUTS

A Knees-Up, Wheels-Up Chronicle of WW II

By J. Douglas Harvey

McCLELLAND AND STEWART

The Canadian Publishers
McClelland and Stewart Limited
25 Hollinger Road
Toronto, M4B 3G2

Canadian Cataloguing in Publication Data

Harvey, J. Douglas, 1922-
   Boys, bombs, and brussels sprouts

ISBN 0-7710-4048-2

1. World War, 1939-1945 – Aerial operations,
Canadian.   2. World War, 1939-1945 – Personal
narratives, Canadian.   3. Harvey, J. Douglas, 1922-
4. Canada.   Royal Canadian Air Force – Biography.
5. Air pilots, Military – Canada – Biography.
I. Title.

D792.C2H37   940.54 '4971 '0924   C81-095046-4

Printed and bound in Canada by
T. H. Best Printing Company Limited

For Our Children

Contents

Did I really drop 68,000 pounds of bombs on Berlin?

Show me the damage.

Did I really boo a man called Mackenzie King?

Who was he?

Did I really make love to a girl on top of a barrage balloon?

Where is the balloon?

Where is the girl?

Was there a bunch of Canadian kids who flew bombers night after night, over Germany?

Does anyone know?

There is no official history of Canada's only bomber force, called No. 6 Group.

This book is not an attempt to correct that historical lapse. The humour, the foolishness, the pettiness, the cowardice, the terror, the stupidity, the ignorance, the shame, and the lust of men seldom, if ever, appear in official military histories.

Over There

The contributions made by Canadian bomber crews in World War Two have never been acknowledged and are little known or appreciated.

Little, if anything, has been written about the only bomber force Canada ever had – No. 6 Group of the Royal Canadian Air Force. Most Canadians have never realized that in World War Two the Royal Canadian Air Force was the world's fourth largest air force and No. 6 Group its largest fighting component.

Canadians should know. They should know the valiant deeds and magnificent achievements of the young men and women who so splendidly upheld the spirit and courage their fathers had shown in World War One. These young Canadians, who carried the old traditions into a new form of battle in the aerial war over Europe, set standards of bravery that equalled or exceeded anything previously known, and they did it with tremendous *élan*.

In order to set the scene it is important to remember that in 1939 the Royal Air Force had only a few small aircraft classified as bombers and hardly enough crews to man them. The Royal Canadian Air Force had neither. The emphasis, if any, in the early war days, was on fighter aircraft and the defence of Britain against invasion from Germany.

It wasn't until the smoke and flame of Dunkirk, the Battle of Norway, and the Battle of Britain had receded that bombing Europe really became a reality in the thoughts of the military planners. The moral arguments over the inhuman nature of bombing cities, debated so fiercely in the British Parliament and in the British press, finally found resolution in the people's desire to give something back. (The arguments, however, persisted throughout the war, and indeed are still heard today.) Unable to invade the Continent, the Allies had little opportunity to strike at Germany unless they used bombers. Until the armies were strong enough to cross the Channel the main thrust against Germany would have to be through the air.

Bomber Command, while charged with this enormous responsibility, was given little or no priority. Ill equipped until 1943 it could not do much more than annoy the European coastal ports. Its small Hampden, Whitley, and Wellington bombers hadn't the speed, range, height, size, or navigational equipment to strike at large targets with the force necessary to inflict major damage. Yet they tried and tried again. When they were decimated in daylight raids by the swarming German fighters, they turned to bombing by night. Under cover of darkness they eluded many fighters, but failed to find many targets.

For three long years the bomber force grew slowly. Pathetically slowly. Aircrew and aircraft were needed for coastal squadrons to fight the Battle of the Atlantic and for operations in the Mid and Far East. Fighter Command still held priority with the aircraft factories. There were few large airfields, few training facilities, and very few aircrew. The stalemate, which saw the German and British armies dormant, separated by the Channel, dragged on as Bomber Command slowly gathered its strength.

Canada, which had little more than a paper air force in 1939, some 4,000 all ranks, somehow sent three squadrons to Britain by 1940 and then turned the RCAF into a national air training scheme. The British Commonwealth Air Training Plan, (BCATP), was primarily based in Canada and from its hastily built training schools and airfields came the aircrew who would provide the force needed to tip the scales against Germany.

Today little, if anything, is known about the Canadian effort in the BCATP. Its airfields, scattered across Canada, lie unmarked, built over or unrecognized by the new generations. Unable to join the tiny RCAF in the early war years, Canadians and Americans had enlisted in the RAF and eventually 25 per cent of the force was Canadian while 45 per cent of all Commonwealth flyers were Canadian.

Prior to 1942, as the RCAF built up its strength, the squadrons it formed in England flew as part of the RAF. But the growing demand for recognition of the Canadian war effort, first by the

Canadian Army, who wanted their own leaders and some control, and then by Canadians in general, led to the formation of the RCAF's own bomber group.

On January 1, 1943, the RCAF formed No. 6 Bomber Group, collecting its squadrons from the RAF. Eventually it consisted of fifteen heavy bomber squadrons, located two to a base on seven airfields in Yorkshire, the northeast corner of England. The RCAF's Pathfinder squadron, No. 405, was located south of the group at Gransden Lodge.

Like the RAF, the RCAF flew British made aircraft, the small twin-engined Hampdens, Whitleys, and Wellingtons, but not the giant four-engined Stirlings. Experienced Canadian aircrew transferred from the RAF to lead the newly formed squadrons.

As the ground stalemate continued, Britain looked more and more, if reluctantly, to Bomber Command for its offensive weapon. The massive build-up of bases, supplies, crews, and aircraft began slowly, since the other services fought viciously over the desperately short supply items and skills then available. It was only when Air Vice-Marshal Arthur Harris took command in late 1942 that Bomber Command became a visible fighting force.

An Englishman who had spent some early years in Rhodesia, this career RAF airman devoted himself day and night for the rest of the war to one single-minded purpose – the destruction of Germany. His determination was unequalled by any Allied commander. Winston Churchill and his Cabinet had little faith in bombers nor did they relish the constant moral questions raised in the House of Commons about bombing civilians. But time and events were on Harris' side. Hitler had turned his attention towards Russia; the aircraft factories were finally turning out four-engined bombers; and the flow of aircrew from the training schools began reaching Britain. Research boffins had focussed their talents to invent airborne radar, bigger and better bombs, and more accurate means of navigation.

Perhaps the greatest ally Harris had, although unwittingly, was Stalin, who was demanding that Britain invade Europe to relieve the German pressure against Russia. Unable to invade Europe by sea, Churchill gave more and more support for Harris' bombers. It took until mid-1943 for Harris to build Bomber Command into a believable force.

The year that began in March 1943 and ended in March 1944,

brought the bloodiest and most devastating aerial battles of any war yet fought. It gave airpower the awesome respect it still holds today. But the price in aircrew lives was enormous. Over 2,700 bombers were shot down and 19,000 aircrew lost in that dreadful year.

Two major German cities, Hamburg and Berlin, were literally removed from the earth, and the Ruhr Valley of industrial cities was levelled from end to end. Hamburg was attacked on four summer nights during July and August. The bombings were called fire raids by the press, but later, when the total devastation became known, the attack was renamed Gomorrah. The Battle of Berlin consisted of sixteen full-effort attacks, with an average of 800 four-engined bombers used on each raid. Berlin, too, was virtually destroyed from the air.

At that time I knew nothing of Harris' grand design or of the horrible ordeal that lay ahead of me. His goal was the total aerial destruction of Germany. My goal, like that of the other kids in Bomber Command was quite simple: to complete thirty raids, the magic number that constituted a tour of operations.

Our lives to this time had been very simple ones. The great Depression of the thirties had made sure of that. It had moulded the innocent youth of Canada in drab parochial ways difficult to imagine in today's world. When the opportunity came to escape that humdrum existence we were ecstatic.

We sprang from all corners of Canada, mostly from schools or the ranks of the unemployed, our eagerness to fly fanned by the heroic exploits of pilots in the Battle of Britain, and our rush to volunteer overwhelmed the tiny peacetime RCAF. As school-aged kids we fought the war in our own style. A style that included a sense of fun and foolishness that brought grace to the business of dying for a cause.

When I joined 408 "Goose" squadron in June 1943, I had exactly 459 flying hours in my log book. I was a sergeant pilot entrusted at age twenty with a crew of six others and destined to fight in the bloodiest air battles ever fought.

What was it like?

Old World, New Ways

Most of the eighteen- and nineteen-year-old Canadian kids who went to war were incredibly naive by any standard. Not only about the war and the world but about much simpler things. Sex, for instance. It can never be determined how many aircrew died in a virgin state, but it was undoubtedly a very high percentage. The English girls must have thought a flock of eunuchs had landed in their midst. Nevertheless they were delighted to meet us and that was quite evident.

My friend Norman Bruce and I went to our first dance soon after arriving in England in 1942. We stayed so late that we missed the bus and had to walk the ten miles back to base. On the way we discussed the evening and in particular the English girls. Norman talked about a dark haired girl he had danced with several times, and one who I remembered as cute.

"She took me outside to neck. God, she was all over me! Could she ever neck. Talk about kissing. . . . Say, have you ever french-kissed a girl?"

"What's that mean?"

"You don't know?" Norman looked at me suspiciously.

"No, I don't. Honest."

"You put your tongue in the girl's mouth."

"Ecch, you did that to her?"

"No, for cripes sake. She did it to me."

"Yeah? She did?" I stopped walking to make sure I heard right. "What was it like?"

"Well, it was, well, not bad, I guess. But that's not all she did." Norman hesitated.

"What else? What did she do?" I urged him.

"She took my hand and put it inside her blouse. Right on her bare tit."

"Oh, God," I moaned. "Are you kidding? On her bare tit? What did you do?"

"I tried to get my hand out but she was holding it there with both of her hands. I was tugging and she was grabbing and finally she let go and ran inside the dance hall. But she never looked at me after that."

We began walking again and neither of us spoke for a long time.

"You know," Norman said, "I think these English girls are different from our Canadian girls."

Norman and I weren't the only kids who went to war in adolescent bliss.

Ken Davidson, our mid-upper gunner, was from Moosomin, Saskatchewan. He was a farm boy who had left high school to enlist in the RCAF; a good looking, well set-up kid with a huge grin and a bright shock of blond hair. He fascinated me with his tales of Prairie farm life: like the time his father had wanted to castrate a huge boar. The pig had grown so big and ugly he was afraid to touch it – until it got caught in a fence and couldn't get out. Ken and his father took a straight razor to the boar, which did the job and freed the pig from the fence, all at the same time.

Then there was the Saturday he was helping his father get ready for spring planting. With four horses pulling a wide-level disc, Ken rounded a corner of a field and hit some stony ground. The frightened horses bolted, two on each side of a barbed wire fence, and they rolled up the fence for a quarter of a mile before Ken could get them stopped.

"What did your dad say?" I inquired.

"Oh, the old man didn't say much. He just asked, 'Son, isn't there a ball game on in town?' "

One night, returning from a raid over Germany, we were forced to land our Halifax S Sugar at an airfield in southern England. We were too low on fuel to reach our base in the north. It was three o'clock in the morning. The duty officer told us he had no beds available and to sleep in the sergeants' mess.

Entering the deserted building with its odour of stale beer and smelly cigarette butts we found some couches and easy chairs. The best couch, a huge leather creation, was occupied by the largest dog I had ever seen: a Great Dane, snoring away with its head draped over one end and its huge ugly hind feet hanging over the other. It was a formidable sight and I had no intention of disturbing its slumbers.

Ken, however, went straight for the dog. He gave it a great whack with his leather flying jacket, yelling, "Get the hell out of here!" The dog sprang up howling and went yelping off, its tail between its legs. "That's better," said Ken, putting on his jacket and nestling into the couch.

Living and flying with a crew put all sorts of personalities together. At the Operational Training Unit we were introduced to four-engined bombers and also to a gang of other kids: navigators, wireless operators, gunners, bomb aimers, and flight engineers. No one was "crewed up" until he had flown in mixed crews for a few weeks. Then it sorted itself out and you formed groups through socializing and flying together. You either liked the look of a guy or you didn't. If you didn't then either you wouldn't fly with him or vice versa.

Ken was only eighteen and very gullible about most things. Growing up on a farm had given him a great zest for living and a fine healthy body, but a little city living would have rounded off the edges. When he joined our squadron he had a total of six months' RCAF service.

During the operational briefings before a bombing raid the medical officer handed out barbiturates. We called them "wakey wakey pills." The theory was that a long seven or eight hour flight, in the dark, would put you to sleep. The pills were supposed to prevent that from happening. The Doc always warned, "Don't take your pills until you are airborne." Ken never listened. Not until the night I tried to strangle him.

Bombing raids were often scrubbed at the last minute due to bad weather but by this time Ken had always swallowed a huge handful of pills. Everyone would go back to the barracks and sleep. But not Ken. He would pace the floor, wide awake, and keep the rest of the barracks in an uproar.

"For Christ's sake, go to sleep!"

"Davidson, if you don't go to sleep I'll kill you!"

"Put that bloody light out, you stupid bastard!"

Everyone tried to get him to go to bed but nothing seemed to work and Davidson would continue to pace the floor. The third straight night that this happened I got out of bed and grabbed him.

He soon knew I meant to strangle him. After some heavy wrestling with everyone joining in, he finally got the message. I made him give me his pills at future briefings, and I kept them until we were airborne and well on the way to the target. I never understood why anyone needed to *use* pills. How could anyone fall asleep over enemy territory with every gun on the Continent trying to shoot you down?

The same Ken had little respect for air force authority and his uniform was mostly his own creation – usually a thick turtleneck sweater, no tie, and battledress with the blouse open. Rarely did he wear his hat, and often he wore brown leather loafers in lieu of the standard black oxfords. He did do something about the shoes by dabbing on a small amount of black polish. Which fooled no one.

Late for briefing one afternoon, he was running full tilt past the station headquarters when he was stopped by a roar coming from a ground floor window.

"You there, that man!" roared the voice. "Stop where you are!" Davidson stopped. A form flung the window fully open and stepped through onto the grass. A Wing Commander staff officer, British, and very correct, marched up to the puzzled Davidson.

"Where is your tie, sergeant?" he barked.

"I don't know, sir."

"Where is your shirt, sergeant?"

"I don't know, sir."

"Where is your hat, sergeant?"

"I don't know, sir."

Then, staring down at Davidson's shoes, the Wing Commander bellowed, "By God, those are brown shoes you're wearing!"

Davidson was tiring of the harangue. "Your eyes," he said, "are damn near good enough for aircrew."

Ken finally showed up at briefing and we flew on ops that night but he never mentioned a thing about his chat with the Wing Commander. The next morning I was called into the CO's office for an explanation of why one of my crew was improperly dressed. I remember saying, "I'm not his mother, for Christ's sake! How should I know why he was dressed like that?"

I then received some news. As the pilot and captain of the aircraft I was supposed to be in charge of my crew at all times. I could understand my responsibilities when we were flying but I couldn't grasp how this could work on the ground. Keeping track of a crew, according to the CO, should be the captain's responsibility, even though I had a mixed crew: sergeants and officers. I was a sergeant. On the ground, regulations dictated that I must salute my crew officers, do their bidding, and call them sir. In the air they were to jump when I gave an order. How insane!

Of course few aircrew paid any attention to this, or did any saluting; and for the majority of the crews, who were all fast friends, there was no rank between them. Everything was on a first name basis. Still, official orders demanded the difference be observed.

The three officers in my crew lived in permanent barracks, built before the war, right on the airfield. They had separate bedrooms, a kitchen, laundry, and batmen to look after their clothes, polish their shoes, make their beds, and serve up tea or whatever. They could walk the short distance to the officers' mess or to the hangar, and they were paid double our salary.

The sergeants lived off the base, five miles away in a huge country estate called Beningbrough Hall. It had been donated to the government for use during the war, and the RCAF had turned it into an aircrew barracks. It was a huge, rambling, three-storied monster set in beautiful grounds. Its enormous green lawns ran all the way to the Ouse River. It must have been a gorgeous place in peacetime, but before it was turned over to the government it had been stripped of all furnishings and its paintings were boarded over. Our "bedroom" consisted of a room fifty feet long on the second floor. A row of iron cots stretched along each wall separated by a ten foot aisle down the centre. The floors were bare wood. No cupboards, no dressers, not even a hook on the wall. You kept your clothes in a duffle bag beside your bed. The mattress was the standard RAF issue: three equally thin squares of canvas that sat on the wire springs. No human could possibly sleep through a night without his ass ending up on the bare, cold springs as the three squares slipped to the floor. There was only one bathroom for twenty-five men. Ah, but the bathtub. A huge seven foot crater! The only time I was ever warm in an English winter was when immersed to the chin in that tub. Government regulations prohibited the use of more than five inches of hot water. The frozen young Canadians said, "Balls," and plunged in to their necks.

Transportation from our barracks to the base was infrequent

and rarely coincided with aircrew requirements that saw you sleeping irregular hours. It was walk in the rain or walk in the mud or walk in those clammy thirty degree temperatures that are colder than any arctic weather. When you finally arrived on base and went to find your officer crew members they were cosily asleep in their private quarters, their personal batmen hovering around. We did the same job but they got double our pay and decent accommodation. It was difficult to understand.

I was captain of my crew, said the CO, and I must look after them. Bullshit. I couldn't go into the officers' mess to socialize with them nor could they come into our sergeants' mess. That was the reason the messes, except for special nights, were empty. The crews, officers and sergeants, went to the local pubs to be together.

The longer I spent in Beningbrough Hall, sharing a bathroom with twenty-five others and living without the least amenities, the more bitter I became towards a system that rewarded some more than others for the same duty. It was galling to wait wearily in the rain for the always delayed lorry to take you home after a raid, while your officers strolled to their private quarters. We sergeants bounced our way home to an iron cot on the floor of a truck. I resented it. Only a few hours before I had led my crew, giving orders and demanding instant obedience. I had been getting the officers to perform specific functions, with their very lives, for a great part, in my hands. But as soon as I landed I reverted to a subservient role. I couldn't understand such a stupid system.

Opportunities for the CO to harp at me for neglecting my crew responsibilities seemed to keep happening. An episode with Jock, our flight engineer, gave the CO another fit.

Sergeant Jock Mabon had joined our crew when Harry, our original flight engineer, had decided after seven trips that he had had enough terror and quit. At age twenty-two Jock was now our oldest crew member. He came from Glasgow and had worked his way up in the RAF from groundcrew by training as a flight engineer. He had a thick Scottish accent and his favourite response was "reet." Which I took to mean "right." Any question directed to him in the aircraft always brought that same reply. "We're all reet, lad." Or, "It's all reet, lad." We all liked Jock.

Jock failed to show up for briefing one evening and so, being short an engineer, we couldn't take off. The CO was furious with me. He demanded to know: what kind of a captain was I? Why couldn't I keep track of my crew? I hadn't a clue where Jock might be and couldn't care less. As far as I was concerned his whereabouts had nothing to do with me. When the CO wanted me to find Jock and bring him to his office early the next morning, I wondered what the hell all the service police were doing. I shouldn't have wondered out loud for it fuelled the blast I was getting.

The next morning, after talking to several of Jock's friends, I headed for the city of York. Someone had given me the address of Jock's girlfriend. She might know where he was. I arrived at a house in a long line of row houses all shouldered together and looking bleak in the rain. I rapped on the door and it came open almost immediately. I was greeted by a ruddy-cheeked middle-aged woman wearing an apron over a flowered house dress. She had a nice smile on her face.

"Hello, what can I do for you?" she asked.

I introduced myself and said, "I'm looking for a sergeant by the name of Jock Mabon. Someone said you might know where he is."

"Oh," she said, beaming, "he's upstairs in bed with Rosie. I'm just taking them a cup of tea. Come along up." She opened the door wider and I followed her as she picked a tray off the stairs and proceeded up.

We entered a bedroom near the top of the stairs with the lady saying, "Hello, look who I've brung to see you." There was Jock, nicely tucked into bed with a rather chubby, smiling blonde girl. They seemed delighted to see me!

"Well lad," said Jock, "everything all reet? Sit down and have a cup of tea with us."

I have been embarrassed before and since but never have I felt it more acutely. "Thanks Jock, but I can't stay. We're flying tonight and the old man is furious. We had to cancel out last night and he wants to see you first thing."

"Fine lad, I'll come right along. Oh, this is Rosie." Jock turned towards the girl.

"How do you do," smiled Rosie. "I'm pleased to meet you."

With the mother beaming and chattering behind me I fled down the stairs. It took about an hour before I realized that I had been the only one embarrassed.

The Wrong Sort Of Flak

Embarrassment, it seemed to me, was a constant way of life in those early war days. I knew I was extremely self-conscious, not to mention unworldly. All I wanted to do was fly an airplane. I had never thought about commanding anyone or being responsible for a crew when I had joined the service. All I wanted to do was fly and fight Germans.

Now suddenly they expected me, a sergeant, to order a crew around and control the actions of my officers. None of the training I had received fitted me for anything but flying an aircraft, and I wanted no part of their system.

Perhaps if I had been more self-confident I could have accepted the absurd idea that a sergeant pilot had authority over an officer in the air, where the officer's life was at stake, but not on the ground, where it wasn't.

My failure to accept this system led to my own personal war on this and other stupidities that made war service so maddening. My self-consciousness started the day I donned a uniform and stepped outside a barracks for the first time. I felt that every eye in the world was watching me. I determined to uphold the traditions of the service, even if I didn't know what they were.

It was a Sunday when I finally got permission to leave Manning Depot at Toronto's Canadian National Exhibition grounds. No one was allowed out during his first week of indoctrination and the wait seemed an eternity. I was dying to get home and dazzle my parents with a real military presence.

The Toronto Transportation Commission (TTC), allowed servicemen in uniform to ride free on Sundays. God bless the TTC but why didn't they tell me? Terribly anxious about my appearance, I boarded a westbound streetcar and tried to shove a ticket into the fare box. The driver beat me to it and clamped his hand over the box.

"This is Sunday," he said.

"So?"

"Everybody in uniform rides free on Sundays."

The car was filled and I was aware of the stares from the passengers, who sat watching and listening and waiting for the car to move on.

"Great," I said. "Give me a transfer, please."

The driver stared at me. "Look," he said, "you don't need a ticket on Sundays."

"Yeah, okay, you said that. But I'll need a transfer when I change cars," I said impatiently, holding out my hand.

"*You don't need a ticket on Sundays.*" He bit off each word in a loud clear voice that carried the length of the streetcar.

"But I'll need a trans – " I began, and then stopped as, finally, the message registered. Blushing furiously I turned to get a seat and found the passengers snickering and elbowing each other. Oh, Jesus, how could I be so stupid and in uniform, too. I scuttled to the rear of the car and slumped into a seat. My first venture into the world as an airman, a magnificent flop.

The uniform issued to you on the first days of service was a disaster, even if it fitted. It was the pants that gave the most trouble. The cloth was so thick and hairy it was difficult to get a crease to hold. The legs weren't wide enough to slide over a knitting needle. And they had button flys.

As soon as we could, we all headed for the tailor shops on Yonge Street. Here they would widen the trouser legs by sewing wedges in the inside pant seams, and put in zipper flys. You huddled in a small booth while the tailor made the alterations. Now you could get your pants on over your huge military boots.

Several of us decided to go to the movies after leaving the tailor shop and we marched up Yonge Street, trying out our best salutes on any officer we could find. Shows were always jammed in those days, and the movies ran continuously from morning to night to accommodate the thousands of young trainees. Getting a seat in the theatre was never a question of where-should-we-sit, but there's-one-seat-up-front. That day I landed in the centre section, halfway between aisles and immediately next to a middle-aged lady wearing a large floppy hat.

I had just gotten interested in the movie when I noticed this lady, out of the corner of my eye, getting ready to leave. She was gathering her coat and purse. As she rose from her seat, I also had to rise in order to let her pass, and as I rose, half standing and half sitting, I noticed that my new zipper fly was open. Hurriedly, I grabbed the zipper and yanked it up, just as the lady brushed in front of me. *Snip.* My zipper caught in the back of her dress. Tugging furiously, I tried to get the dress free; but as the lady moved along the row the material tightened and I was pulled along behind her, still in a half crouch, stumbling over the feet of the other people. I was still struggling desperately when we reached the aisle, and the lady suddenly became aware of a presence behind her. She began to hurry towards the door, and I had to bend over double to keep up with her. Meanwhile, she was throwing ferocious looks over her shoulder as I stumbled at her heels. Terrified at the thought of what might happen if she started to scream, I gave a mighty yank on the zipper and her dress came free. But not before we had entered the brightly lit lobby where hundreds of people were waiting to enter the show. What they thought of a young airman, who seemed to be pulling the dress off a lady, I'll never know. I fled back to barracks in a cold sweat, thankful that I had escaped her wrath.

Every airman who went through the RCAF's Manning Depot – and nearly a hundred thousand did – remembers the "bull pen." It was our first air force home. A huge area, it was occupied once a year by the Royal Winter Fair and then, indeed, it housed bulls and not a few cows. Countless rows of double decker bunks stretched from end to end of this sea of a building. Here, a blue kit bag beside your bunk, you endured the orientation from civvy to military life.

Thousands of kids away from home for the first time in their young lives. . . . Kids from Newfoundland, Texas, New York, the Prairies, Quebec, the Maritimes, even the Yukon, were jammed into the bull pen. Four needles plus a vaccination scratch at one swift application and then, arms swollen, you tried to climb into an upper bunk.

Fights every night as soon as the lights went off at ten o'clock sharp. . . . A voice calling in the dark, "I'm from Texas and I can beat the shit out of any stupid Canadian." Bunks scraping back to form a ring, as a challenger rose to do battle. Another voice calling out, "Anybody here from the West?" Every voice responding in a mighty chorus, "Fuck the West!"

Money belts, of course in air force blue, sold like hotdogs. Petty thievery was rife among the seventy-five cents a day recruits, and when and if the culprit was caught stealing, he was dealt with by a "drumming out" parade. It was horrible and mandatory to watch the punishment. The entire station paraded into a hollow square and there, to the roll of drums, the thief was stripped, button by button, by a huge sword wielded by the CO. Then the cap and tunic belt were flipped off. The charge was read and the victim was marched off parade and out of the service. Dishonourably discharged. It left the desired impression and thievery dropped, until the next time.

Learning to salute was taught each and every day. With the fingers of the right hand extended, bring your right arm up, straight out from your body, and then bring your right hand smartly to the edge of your right eye. Remember, the longest way up, the shortest way down. Salute.

The instructors, those infamous corporals, were very good at teaching us how to salute, but they never bothered to tell us *who* to salute. Then you received a blast when you saluted them. "You only salute officers, for Christ's sake!" How did we know an officer? We had barely seen one and the rank system was a great mystery yet to be solved. So we saluted everything that moved. Always in doubt, we adhered to the age old military dictum: "If you see something, salute it. If it doesn't salute back, pick it up. If you can't pick it up, paint it." Finally you could march in step and salute, and were posted to guard duty for more ground pounding activity as you waited impatiently to do the only thing you wanted. To fly.

St. Thomas is located in southwestern Ontario, not far from London and smack in the farming district. It was here the RCAF took over an institutional building and opened a cooking school. Thousands of airmen and airwomen were trained as cooks and chefs and chefs' helpers at St. Thomas. It was a depressing place with little spirit or imagination. The grounds were surrounded by tall wire fences topped with barbed wire. Sentry boxes had been erected at each of the fence corners. They stood about twenty feet high and here, rifle in hand, we would perch four hours on and four hours off, on guard duty.

Security of the base was vital, we were told. The Germans might attack at any time. How we all wished they would, if only to taste the food, dished up by former farmers, lumberjacks, and miners. Long weaving lines of airmen bent themselves into figure eights, as they waited their turn at the smelly steamtables and a chance to sample the delicacies prepared by those novice cooks. Service was so slow that people had time to scrawl messages or slogans on the red brick walls of the mess hall. Paraphrasing was a popular pastime.

"Never in the field of human conflict, have so many waited so long, for so little." There were other shorter and sharper messages. Their pithy comments were directed to the cook and all offered advice on just where the wretched person should place his or her burned offerings. The hardboiled eggs, served at every breakfast, were actually bounced like tennis balls to the dining tables!

Guard duty was the place we all learned what every recruit in history learns. Never volunteer. Following each morning's parade, the day's duties were detailed for those not standing immediate guard.

"Can anyone read music?"

"Yes, sir, I can," a voice would pipe up from the ranks.

"Don't call me sir!" the corporal would roar. "Fall out and report to the sergeant at the officers' mess. Does anyone have a licence to drive a car?"

A chorus of voices. "Yes, I have."

"You, you, and you," the corporal would point. "Fall out and report to the transport section. . . . Has anyone here done any woodworking?"

"Yes, sir, I have."

"Don't call me sir, for Christ's sake! I'm a corporal. I may look like an officer but I only have two stripes!" The corporal would scream this at the man while pointing to his sleeve and his two stripes. "Fall out and report to the mess hall."

It went on until all had been assigned a duty, everyone eager to avoid real work and get a chance to do something of interest. The musical genius would turn up at the officers' mess – to find he was expected to move the grand piano to the recreation hall. Volunteers would arrive at the motor transport section, clutching their drivers' licences, only to be handed buckets and told to wash the CO's car. The woodworker would find himself on his knees, on a large wooden floor, scrub brush in hand. The corporal's ruses always worked.

Life was firmly in the corporal's hands. Except for those times the service police had a chance to show authority.

"You there, that man! Where do you think you are going?" Bewildered, a forty-eight hour pass clutched firmly in your hand, you stopped, as the service police challenged you at the camp gate.

"I'm going on a forty-eight hour pass . . . sir."

"Not with hair like that, you're not. Get a haircut."

"But corporal, I had a haircut this morning."

"Well, this time tell the barber to take some hair off your head." Back to the barber shop, hoping it was still open. Every unemployed man of any Canadian town situated near a military base in 1940, could get a job cutting hair. No one ever made so much money, in so short a time. They had all, we believed, been trained by Australian sheep shearers and were unmatched in their skill with electric clippers.

"Next." The long line shuffled forward a step. *Flap,* went the hairy sheet around your neck. *Zap,* went the electric clippers. *Snap*, went the sheet. "Next."

When the service police were really enjoying life, they would send you back for yet another haircut, as you tried to get through the gate.

"But I've just had a haircut, corporal. You sent me there half an hour ago."

"Get a haircut or forget about your pass."

Bastard. Just wait. The day will come when you are still a corporal and I'm a sergeant and then you'll get yours. I dreamed of the day I would repay those martinets. There was one corporal in particular who had cancelled four of my weekend passes. He kept me scrubbing the same floor, over and over, all day Saturday and all day Sunday, on four consecutive weekends. I really did dream about him. But it was over a year later before my dream came true.

I had been on the squadron several months when I bumped into him, rounding a corner of the hangar. Immersed in my thoughts I didn't recognize him as we collided. It wasn't until he spoke that I realized who he was. God, it can't be true. Corporal Wilson! My blood raced. He looked down at my sleeve where the crown signified I was a warrant officer. I looked at his sleeve and his corporal's stripes. Now you son of a bitch, we'll see about all those floors.

But all we did was socialize and exchange pleasantries. It had been too long ago and my hatred was buried in days that seemed eons old. I never saw him after that nor did I ever think about my lost opportunity. I was enduring another form of torture that was far more important.

All of the pettiness vanished from our training as soon as we were posted to Elementary Flying School. Now we were going to learn how to fly, and we bent every effort to master the renowned Tiger Moth. The anxiety and worry that filled every aircrew trainee seems unreal today. What if I get airsick? What if I fail to solo? What if I fail the twenty hour check ride? What if I can't do a roll to the right? We knew that over 25 per cent of all pilots were being washed out. Sometimes entire courses were washed out and sent for retraining as air gunners or navigators or bomb aimers. We just had to get our pilots' Wings. Still more important, we just had to get overseas. Damn those ground school exams and damn that miserable flying instructor who couldn't see how good a pilot you were. Our motivation came from within. No one needed to coerce us. There were no pep talks on how badly pilots were needed to fight the war. They weren't necessary. We read the papers. We knew Hitler was stomping through country after country; was rounding up Jews. We knew Sailor Malan had just knocked down a Focke-Wulf 190, to score his twentieth victory. We knew that Buzz Beurling, the kid from Verdun, Quebec, was shooting Germans and Italians out of the sky over Malta, his Spitfire a formidable threat to enemy formations. God, how great it all seemed . . . if you could only get your Wings.

Finally, the grand day. Wings parade. No other parade was as significant as the day you stepped forward to have those coveted Wings pinned on your tunic. Then the big question: where were you posted? Not (you hoped) as an instructor in Canada. Not to a Canadian coastal squadron. Not as a staff pilot in Canada. Hurray, you were posted overseas!

"You're a lucky bastard," said Wing Commander Dave Hard-ing, as he pinned on my Wings. "Put me in your pocket and take me with you." I smiled, indulgently, feeling a trifle sorry for those unfortunates left behind in Canada.

Halifax and the "Y" Depot. We were finally on our way. Excited beyond words we waited for our overseas draft to be assigned a ship. No ordinary ship for us. We were loaded aboard the *Queen Elizabeth*. Was all this real? We were going overseas on the world's largest ship. But then, so were about 20,000 other guys and gals. The huge ocean liner had been stripped of all luxury fittings; her cabins and state rooms were converted into barracks and her monstrous decks lined with double decker bunks. Faster than any ocean liner afloat, the *Queen* needed no convoy to escort her across the Atlantic. Zigging and zagging she could make the trip in four days from Halifax or New York to England or Scotland.

On board we were assigned quarters that in peacetime would have been a single cabin in the second class section. Bunks, four tiers high, accommodated eighteen men. Sixteen of our room mates were Norwegian Air Force pilots who had trained at "Little Norway" in Toronto. On deck we found the Irish Regiment of Canada and their famous pipe band. The Thirty-eighth Sportsmen's Battery organized and commanded by Major Connie Smythe, bustled about getting settled into bunks lashed on the open decks. There was Gunner Ted Reeve, Canada's premier sportswriter on the double, his great army boots thudding down the gangways as he carried out orders. There was Sergeant Ed Houston, his new navigation badge shining, destined to be a prisoner of war for two years and later a judge and esteemed member of Canada's Law Reform Commission.

Four wonderful days as the great *Queen* steamed at thirty knots, forever turning to avoid detection by the lurking subs. Beautiful nights on the fantail as the Irish Guards performed concerts and led the enormous sing-songs. Visits to the fantastic engine room. Around the clock crap games, poker, and bridge. Huge mess tables thirty feet long, with cooks sliding great pans of food down their polished lengths. The RAF kids who had trained in Canada, gorging on the last decent food they would taste. The Norwegians lying in their bunks masturbating for all the world to see, so that you walked the decks whether you wanted to or not. Some people were out of their quarters most of the time. Constant rumours of

U-boat sightings lent credence to popular belief that the ship would be attacked in the middle of the night, and the believers, lifejackets secure, slept on the open decks.

But one impressive sight brought us all to line the rails. The green hills of Scotland. We were overseas!

Wild Colonial Boys

We went immediately by train to Bournemouth on the south coast of England; a seven hour ride. Here the RCAF had taken over some hotels, and used them to house all newly arrived airmen. It was a holding unit that allowed the different trades to be sorted out and fed into the various training pipelines. It was here we spent our first two months waiting for postings to flying units. Impatient, bored, already homesick, tired of the constant parades and make-work schedules, we yearned for an aircraft.

Bournemouth had been closed to its normal tourist business, and nearly all the large hotels were taken over by the military for use as barracks. The seaside promenade was closed and huge rolls of barbed wire stretched along the sea front. But a few English vacationers could still be seen. They were older, retired couples, who wandered about, wrapped to their chins in heavy tweeds, caps, and scarfs, the men wearing plus fours and swinging walking canes. They returned our stares, as bewildered about us as we about them.

Completely bored, I roamed the town but found little of interest. When are they going to post us out of here to a flying station? We all asked that question each day. There wasn't much to divert my attention. Nineteen years old, a non-smoker, non-drinker, a girlfriend back in Canada, I was locked in a town that catered to retirees.

Norman Bruce had been a schoolmate in Toronto. We had joined the RCAF together and somehow managed to stay together through all our various training courses. The two of us wandered around Bournemouth completely out of our element. Our biggest concern was learning how to count the English money. Pounds, shillings, and pence made no sense to either of us. Our usual practice when buying something in the shops was to put all our money in our hand and let the shopkeeper take what he wanted. In this way we were able to pay a pound for twelve wire coat hangers, although it took two days to figure out we had been gypped.

One of the games we invented to distract ourselves was rolling the large English pennies down the hilly streets of Bournemouth in order to see who could roll them the farthest. Each penny weighed a ton. Our childish game was often ruined by the English gentry strolling about. They would trot after the pennies at the bottom of the hill and then, to our amazement, labour up the slope to return them. With sidelong, mirthful glances we would roll them down again, to their utter consternation.

Finally, the postings: you were posted to RAF station Church Lawford. Where the hell is that? What kind of aircraft do they fly? Nobody in authority knew or cared. Church Lawford turned out to be an advanced flying unit, located near the town of Rugby. We all knew about Rugby and its famous school from the English comic books we had grown up reading. Now our education into all things Royal Air Force was to begin.

The tiny English train dumped twenty-five RCAF pilots, including a half dozen American kids, at a grubby station platform in the middle of the night. We were told to jump in the back of a lorry with our kit bags, which held our total worldly goods. After many jolting miles the truck stopped near a row of tin huts, surrounded by a sea of mud. A sergeant barked out names and we were assigned, twelve to a hut. Not just a hut. A Nissen hut. The name surely lives in infamy with everyone unfortunate enough to have occupied this modern-day version of the igloo.

An Englishman, by the name of Lord Nissen, had invented a metal hut, considered a marvel of British engineering. It was enthusiastically adopted by the military in two world wars as the answer to housing troops. It was cheap. Hundreds of thousands of them were erected all over Britain. No building in history has been so loathed. Why the poor man ever allowed his name to be associated with the structure is something I fail to comprehend. When he died in 1943, the newspapers carried his obituary in bold type. I carried the clipping around for the rest of the war, disappointed that I never had a chance to personally congratulate him on the legacy he had left the troops.

The Nissen hut was nothing more than a concrete pad over which corrugated iron sheets were bolted in a continuous arch from one side to the other. The end walls were made of wood. A door and two tiny windows were located at one of the ends. It was large enough to house a row of six iron cots on either side of a centre aisle, which was the only spot where you could stand fully erect. Heat was supposedly supplied by a tiny iron stove, erected in and blocking the centre aisle. A short length of stove pipe ran through the tin roof to allow the choking clouds of smoke to escape. It wasn't very effective since the soft, oily lumps of coal that were allocated, seven lumps per day, were rain soaked and unburnable. It didn't matter how much coal you stole from the closely guarded coal pile, or how many lumps you rammed into the tiny stove. It was perfectly heat proof.

"Why doesn't somebody light the stove?" a voice would cry out from under its blankets.

"For God's sake," came the answer, "it *is* lit."

"Well put some more coal on the fire."

"I can't get any more into the damn thing."

"Pour some paint dope on the coals."

"I have, and it still won't burn."

But the Nissen hut was very cleverly designed to hold maximum moisture. The tin acted as a conductor that made the inside of the hut damper than the outside. Putting on clothes in the morning, if you had had the courage to remove them the night before, was like putting on a wet bathing suit, only much colder.

It was even colder in the sergeants' mess and not only because the windows were open in the winter. We were the first colonials this RAF base had ever seen. Everyone did their best to ignore us completely. Chilly. It was soon evident to us that we had disrupted their peacetime routine, to which they still stubbornly clung. Our disruption began the very first day when we found a meal being served at four o'clock. Funny time to serve dinner we thought, but dig in, chaps. We were always starving in that cold climate and we proceeded to devour every cake and tart in sight. Not much of a meal, the Yanks among us bitched, but they were as delighted as the Canadians when, at six o'clock, another meal was served. This isn't going to be so bad after all. Two meals every afternoon, boy, we've got it made.

In all fairness it should be said that not one of us knew anything about the English custom of afternoon tea at four o'clock. One, we found, was expected to have a tart or small slice of cake with his tea, not eat every last morsel, wipe out the honey and jam pots with bread, and leave every plate shiny, as we had done. That ended the afternoon tea and the RAF types never forgave us.

A more pleasant surprise at Church Lawford was that our flying instructors turned out to be the greatest. Many of them were pre-war officers holding permanent ranks, and most had flown on operations in the 1939-40 "phoney war," dropping leaflets over Germany. They were now firmly ensconced at a training base and here they wished to remain for the duration. Huge handle-bar mustaches prevailed, and so did the mile and a half of woollen scarf looped around their necks. To us Canadian kids they looked medieval, and we stared at them in wonder as we tried to decipher the mumbles and coughs that passed for speech.

We didn't laugh at them in the air. Oh, but they were great instructors! It was here that many of us really learned what flying was all about. They introduced us to something called an Airspeed Oxford, something similar to the twin-engined Avro Anson we had flown in Canada. But the Oxford was even flimsier and looked like it was made from orange crates. My first flight in one was supposed to be a flip around the area of Church Lawford; an orientation flight to get used to the machine and to learn from the air where we were stationed. Church Lawford didn't have runways since it was a grass aerodrome. The grass had been painted with large, black, swirling lines which resembled hedges when seen from the air. It was my first experience with camouflage and I found it very effective as I floated in to land, goosing the engines to clear a hedge that turned out to be a painted line on the grass.

On this familiarization flight my instructor became bored with explaining the various landmarks and turned the controls over to me with a, "Have a go, old chap. Try a few stalls and wring it out a bit."

After a two month absence from the controls of an aircraft I was a bit rusty and hamfisted. I yanked off the throttles and jerked the stick back hard – too hard – to make it stall. *Flick*, the aircraft did a snap roll. Alarmed, I turned to the instructor. "What the hell happened?" To myself I said, this aircraft is unstable.

"I say, I think the old girl went completely around," he muttered unconcernedly. "Here, let me have a go." When he tried, the Oxford fell into a meek stall. "Amazing," he said, and the matter wasn't mentioned again. It served to set the tone for the RAF training that rounded off the edges left from the more frantic RCAF flying instructors. The unflappable British were the last word in instrument flying and totally relaxed in the foulest weather, weather we had never been permitted to fly in previously. They taught us how to fly on instruments with utter confidence and they made up for all the ludicrous orders, antics, and petty snobbishness of the CO and his ground staff.

Church Lawford was full of Italian soldiers, prisoners from the North African campaign. They wore their brown uniforms as they laboured at various jobs around the airfield. Each had been issued a bicycle, and they would come streaming down the camp roads, 100 at a time, all singing at the top of their voices and saluting everything they passed. Many were still deeply tanned from the African sun which made their smiles visible for yards. They must have been the happiest prisoners anywhere. No one seemed to know anything about them. Where they lived, where they ate, and who was responsible for them remains a mystery to me to this day.

Bicycles were also part of our lives from the first day at Church Lawford. Since transportation was a major problem on every airfield, it was standard practice to issue bicycles to the airmen so they could come and go to the hangars. What the authorities overlooked was the question of what happened to those bikes at night. Riding a bike at night is dangerous enough but in blacked out England it was often suicidal. We did it anyway.

After a few beers and nothing much else to do, a whole gang of Canadian aircrew would ride out of camp to run races on the main highways. Truck transport in England was very well regulated and each vehicle had a Max Speed sticker stencilled on its fenders proclaiming the speed limit for that particular van or lorry. Most were twenty-five miles per hour stickers. We could, by judiciously timing our runs from the top of a hill, get our bikes up to twenty-five miles an hour and catch those dawdling vans. Which meant a gaggle of guys, heads down, pumping like mad, flying along the road in total darkness. The only lights on the trucks were hooded headlights that cast a small amount of light down and straight ahead. This was one of the major reasons they travelled so slowly. But to us, twenty-five miles an hour seemed like 100 in the dark, and our rides ended in the ditch, a pile of broken spokes and bent and twisted wheels and handle bars, as the truck rounded a curve or swerved to miss strayed farm animals. A lot of bruises, torn uniforms, and chipped teeth later, we would wend our happy way back to base.

If your bike had been smashed it was necessary to exchange it for a serviceable one before retiring. No one ever succeeded in keeping his bicycle more than a few days. Parking in front of the mess was an open invitation for someone to steal your machine. Often the liberator never left a replacement or if he did, it had twisted wheels or flat tires or no tires at all. You then walked around until nightfall and an opportunity to make a decent exchange.

A lot of RAF kids had motorcycles and a few officers hared about in ancient MG's and Austins. Their cars were borrowed so much they got in the habit of removing the rotor from the distributor before leaving it unattended. For the car owners, stealing petrol was a main occupation. Since gas was strictly rationed, the car owners borrowed 100-octane aviation fuel. They also borrowed batteries and even tires from ack trollies used to start aircraft. A car owner needed friends. Not only to pirate parts and gas, but to help push the car when it ran out of gas or blew a tire or got caught in heavy fog. Rarely did a car leave the base without a full load of passengers. With careful cramming it was possible to get eight people in the tiny Austin and often another one or two on the running boards.

Scotty Peck, an American, bought the first car in our group. At least he said he had bought the car; his lifestyle always left you wondering. Scotty had made $5,000 running a crap game aboard our troop ship and he lived high on the hog for nearly a year. He called his car the Mayflower, claiming a lot of girls had come across in it. The rest of us went on dates on our bicycles: the WAAF riding her immaculate machine and you on your bent, twisted, mud covered equivalent.

When we had finished advanced flying training we were split up once more and again friends disappeared, going their separate ways. Many you would never see again. Norman Bruce and I had managed to stay together from the very first day but now our paths separated. He went to one Operational Training Unit and I went to another. We kept in contact by letter for a long time. Eventually he was posted to a Canadian bomber squadron operating in North Africa, while I was posted to 408 squadron at Leeming, Yorkshire.

His letters continued until he was shot down while flying partisans and arms into Yugoslavia. He spent the rest of the war in a German POW camp and was one of those who survived the long death marches from camp to camp. Norman won the Distinguished Flying Medal for his part in the African campaign, something he never mentioned in his letters. They usually concerned themselves with the inanities and stupidities committed by the service in the desert sands of Africa. He wrote to say that the RCAF had asked for 100 aircrew to be sent out from England and they were surprised to receive 100 airscrews. In another letter he told of the army requesting a half million sand bags to bolster their desert fortifications. The bags were sent out from England filled with sand.

Let's Go Fly A Kite

To walk into the squadron gunnery section and listen to the air gunners from all twenty crews, sitting around bullshitting each other, was always a revelation to me.

"You should see my pilot grease our kite onto the runway. He's the best pilot on the squadron."

"My pilot can fly lower than anybody. He can make the water swirl up the props when we low-fly over the sea."

"My pilot never bounces on landing. You don't even know you're on the ground until the aircraft slows down."

"My pilot says he could take our kite off on only one engine. I bet he could, too."

Total confidence. Total trust. Where it came from I'll never know. If you were a pilot yourself, though, you soon discovered who could fly and who couldn't. There were a few on our squadron that I would never fly with. Most of these were former flying instructors from the Canadian training bases, who had flown too long by the book. Training flying and operational flying were two different things. It's interesting to speculate how many crews were shot down because the pilots had spent too much time instructing or believing everything taught them at training schools.

A kid who had trained with me at Service Flying School in Canada was a case in point. He was simply a parrot, repeating back to the instructor everything the instructor wanted to hear and kissing his ass while so doing. When we graduated and received our pilots' Wings he received a commission to Pilot Officer. The top 10 per cent of each pilots' course was commissioned. The remainder received the non-commissioned rank of sergeant. He arrived on our base for his operational tour and rose rapidly to Squadron Leader rank due to the tremendous losses we were suffering. The rest of the guys who had trained with him were, of course, still sergeants or flight sergeants. We had to listen to his lectures on non-flying days.

He gave a lecture on airmanship one day which we were all forced to attend, bored out of our minds. It was tragic. "Remember," he said, "when flying crosswind that your airspeed indicator will read incorrectly." It was difficult to believe an operational pilot could make such a stupid and dangerous remark. Anyone who had taken the most basic flying instruction knew that wind had no effect on the airspeed indicator – only on the ground speed of the aircraft. When we all roared with laughter he became very indignant. He was a Squadron Leader and we were sergeants. How could he be wrong? None of us was really surprised when he was killed a few weeks later. He thought he was landing at our base, but he had lined up on a nearby field and crashed into a hill.

My first operational flight was with a former flying instructor, another Squadron Leader, who was making his thirteenth raid. New pilots, when first posted to a squadron, flew as observers with seasoned crews to get some idea of how to handle things. Since our bombers had only one pilot's seat and one set of controls, the new "sprog" pilot had to sit in the engineer's seat. They were called "second dickie" trips.

The squadron was briefed for a raid on Gelsenkirchen in the Ruhr Valley, referred to by all aircrew as "Happy Valley." Our Halifax Mark II aircraft was underpowered in comparison to later Marks and the largest sized bomb it could carry weighed only 2,000 pounds.

Crossing the French coast, we were manoeuvring through the coastal searchlights and heavy flak when the Squadron Leader noticed the port-outer engine revolution counter was oscillating about 500 revs. On a training flight you would automatically stop the engine to avoid injuring it. That is exactly what he did.

He told me to feather the port-outer. Since this was my first trip and I was there to learn, I reluctantly stopped, or feathered, the engine. Immediately the heavily loaded bomber began losing altitude as we flew towards the target. Soon we could see the searchlights and the flak belting up in great colourful streams with the fires spreading through the city. We had lost height and speed and were now at 14,000 feet as we began our bomb run, the main bomber stream high over our heads. We managed to bomb and escape off the target without getting hit by the German flak or our own falling bombs, and flew towards the darkness and the French coast.

The Squadron Leader had just settled on the homeward course when the rear gunner yelled, "Enemy fighter, six o'clock low, corkscrew starboard, go!" The Squadron Leader had difficulty throwing the Halifax around with only three engines working. Tracer shells began whipping over our port wing. *Bang!* An explosion ripped the port-inner engine and it stopped. As the Squadron Leader wrestled with the crippled bomber I shut off the engine and pressed the fire extinguisher. With only two engines working we lost altitude rapidly and were below 10,000 feet when the mid-upper gunner suddenly yelled, "Enemy fighter coming in at three o'clock, corkscrew starboard, go!"

Pushing the nose down, the Squadron Leader screamed towards the cloud bank below. As we entered the cloud we lost the fighter but the captain was having terrible difficulty holding the Halifax on a straight course. The two engines on the starboard side were now at full power and they pushed the aircraft towards the two dead engines. The rudder trim couldn't correct for the great torque and at the same time there was insufficient power to hold our altitude.

The Squadron Leader ordered me into the pilot's seat with him to try and get some extra leverage on the rudder bars. It was a tight squeeze as I jammed in beside him. I got my left foot on the rudder bar and this helped him hold the course but my leg grew numb from the pressure of locking my leg straight.

We were now down to 1,000 feet and still losing height as the skipper ordered the crew to throw out everything not bolted down. Out went the guns and ammunition, flares, ration box, portable toilet, fire axe, and ladder, as we struggled slowly towards the coast. It looked like we would be forced to ditch in the English Channel, if we could make it that far.

I had wondered why the Squadron Leader wouldn't restart the port-outer engine that we had feathered because of the rev counter oscillation. As a sprog pilot I was reluctant to ask him. He was an experienced captain and was making his thirteenth trip. At the same time, I didn't relish ditching at night. After some soul searching, I finally asked why we couldn't unfeather the port-outer engine.

There was a long, overly long pause, until finally the Squadron Leader said, "Okay, start up the port-outer."

As I got the engine going and brought it up to full power it lifted the port wing. The pressure on the rudder bars returned to normal as the aircraft began climbing. I got out of the pilot's seat and stood in the aisle. Soon, West Malling, a base in southern England showed up, and the Squadron Leader plunked us in there for the night. He received the Distinguished Flying Cross for that night's work. The rest of the crew got nothing.

I never forgot that trip or the valuable lesson I had learned. When your ass is on the line, I reasoned, use everything available. It might hurt an engine to run it when you shouldn't, but an engine can be replaced if you get back. It was great experience for the operational tour I was ready to begin with my own crew.

Our first raid as a full crew took place two nights after I had returned to base with the Squadron Leader's crew. The squadron was briefed to attack Aachen, located at the southern end of the Ruhr Valley. Our own Halifax bomber was unserviceable and we were assigned R Roger. I always hated using another aircraft. It was a superstition I was never able to overcome.

The weather was clear at base but thick clouds stretched across the North Sea and the Continent. I could tell my crew was keyed up and anxious to discover what operational flying was all about. They had questioned me endlessly about my "second dickie" trip, particularly wanting to know what the target looked like under attack.

They were not about to find out on this trip for it was a complete failure. Try as I could, I could not get the Halifax above 15,000 feet. I never understood the reason, for I climbed the aircraft at full throttle almost to the Dutch coast. Too low to cross the coastal defences, I turned back and dropped the bombs in the sea. None of us felt very good about it, especially when our friends returned a few hours later in triumph, ecstatic over their success. While our failure had a marked effect on the crew it actually did much to strengthen my resolve to try harder, to become more professional.

My feelings of inadequacy were soon to disappear as we made five successful raids in the next seven nights. The devastation of

Hamburg had begun and we went there on three nights, interspersed with two attacks on Ruhr Valley targets. Those five raids over so short a time melded our sprog crew into a cohesive whole and did much to convince us all that we could cope. After those raids I never again agonized over our first abortive trip.

Strange Exports

The last of the four fire raids on Hamburg was August 2, 1943. One of the worst storms of the summer coincided with that raid. This, although we didn't know it, was to be our last operational flight in a Halifax bomber. We would retrain on the Lancaster Mark II. It was my seventh trip and I felt I was getting in the groove.

I headed out over the North Sea, flying in solid cloud that contained heavy, clear ice. Our bombers had little protection against ice. Only some de-icing liquid that could be sprayed on the windscreen and propellers, and anti-icing paste that the groundcrew rubbed on the leading edges of the wings. It was not very effective.

With only 500 flying hours recorded in my log book, I hadn't previously encountered severe icing conditions. Since it was night and we were flying in cloud I couldn't see my wings and didn't at first realize the aircraft was icing up so badly. I should have known from the way the Halifax was failing to respond to the controls and refusing to climb. Maximum revs on the Merlin engine were 3,000 and I had been flying at 2,850 revs since leaving base.

The raids on Hamburg marked the first time Bomber Command had used "window" – thin strips of aluminum foil cut to the exact length of the German radar frequency. Each aircraft hurled out bundles of these strips, which separated in the slipstream and fluttered down, totally confusing the radar controlled guns and searchlights. Until the Germans found a way to filter these false signals, their guns were completely out of control. The searchlights swept aimlessly back and forth and the heavy flak guns were unable to get correct range bearings. The Germans finally solved the problem but not before Hamburg was destroyed. The four fire raids, in nine days, began July 24 and ended August 2. Over 60 per cent of the city was destroyed.

The term, fire raid, came from the terrible fires that swept the city. As the incendiary bombs crashed down, the fires reached temperatures of 1,000 degrees. Air was sucked into Hamburg and it bellowed itself into cyclones of flame and smoke that roared through twenty square miles of the city on winds of 150 miles an hour. Thousands were suffocated from lack of oxygen. Their bodies were incinerated in the streets and bomb shelters and in the basements of their homes. More than 40,000 people were killed outright and a million refugees fled from Hamburg. The fires never went out during the nine days it took to drop 9,000 tons of bombs, since each raid increased the inferno.

While the Germans were battling fires, we were being encrusted with ice. As I struggled with the ice-laden bomber to gain altitude it was clear we wouldn't get above 17,000 feet. By dropping the nose slightly and then pulling back on the controls it was often possible to nudge the bomber up fifty feet at a time. But our Merlin engines were in danger of overheating. The glycol gauges showed the temperatures of the coolant already in the red, and my sharp pulls on the controls threatened to stall the aircraft.

Thunderstorms were all around us. Lightning was tearing and streaking through the cumulus nimbus clouds, lighting the sky and making it possible now and then to see what a wild night sat outside the cockpit window. A thing called "Saint Elmo's fire" crackled and danced all across the inside of the windscreen and all over the flying panel. Sparkling blue flames leaped and snaked, making it difficult to concentrate on the instruments. With each lightning bolt I could see the massive thunderclouds surrounding us, some a rosy red from the reflected fires sweeping the city.

Our wireless operator, Ray, an English lad, was positioned near the rear door of the aircraft throwing out bundles of "window." He could hear me cursing the weather and talking to Eric, the navigator, about the way the aircraft was behaving.

Suddenly Ray began to scream, "Turn back, skipper, turn back! We're all going to be killed! Please, skipper, turn back!"

His screams threw panic into everyone and put the hair on the back of my neck straight out. I yelled at him over the intercom to shut up but he kept screaming, his screams getting louder and louder and more hysterical. I ordered the bomb aimer to go back with a fire extinguisher and stop the screaming. Plugging into a portable oxygen bottle, Steve started to crawl towards the rear of the bomber. "Hit the bastard over the head," I ordered.

The screaming continued to grow louder and more frightening and I found it hard to concentrate on flying the Halifax as it wobbled under its load of ice. Suddenly the screaming stopped, and I thought Steve had managed to quiet Ray. But Steve came on the intercom to report that the rear door was open and the wireless operator had baled out. He had jumped without unplugging his intercom which explained the sudden silence.

I shut my mind to the problem as I continued to wrestle with the Halifax. For the last twenty minutes I had been watching a huge cumulus nimbus thunderhead as the lightning outlined its monstrous swollen form. Its anvil shaped top, thousands of feet above our flight level, was drifting across our path.

I knew instinctively that if I got into that thunderhead our wallowing bomber would be in terrible danger. Trying to keep on course and yet avoid the storm, I was inching my way around the storm cloud, or so I thought. Ice on the windscreen and the blue flames crackling on the inside of the window made it difficult to see, and the darkness of the night blended with the black form of the clouds.

Without warning we plunged into the cloud and the bomber stalled. With one wing down, because we had been turning, the aircraft started into a spin, the instruments gone wild and the altimeter needle racing backwards. I knew I might never recover from the spin and ordered the crew to bale out.

Eric was screaming at me to drop the bombs. The harder I pulled back, the tighter the spin became. I slammed the bomb doors open and pulled the bomb jettison handle. The sudden opening of the huge bomb bay doors acted as an airbrake and with the stick hard over and full rudder, the Halifax slowly straightened into a dive. I got control at 5,000 feet but we were still bumping around in the thunderhead.

I called the crew to find them still on board. No one had been able to bale out. The force of gravity in that wild plunge had pinned them into their seats. They all responded as I closed the bomb doors and turned to a compass heading for home.

We had dropped our bombs about ten miles short of the target, which seemed much closer at the lower altitude. The fierce winds associated with the thunderstorms were fanning the flames and the entire city was a Dante's inferno. The ice began melting off the wings at our lower altitude and great chunks started to pound the fuselage, thrown there by the propellers. As our speed slowly returned to normal, I began to climb up to a safer altitude for the long run home across the sea.

It felt strange to head for home without one of the crew. No one mentioned the subject but they must all have wondered if Ray had made it safely to earth. We maintained radio silence and waited until we were back at base before talking about it. Utter terror had obviously seized Ray and overcome his normal reactions. As we flew over the sea I tried to reason what had caused him to jump. He had never exhibited any abnormal behaviour on any previous flight and had performed his chores efficiently and without bitching.

But then, as I sat there in the dark, I began remembering things Ray had said, at least once a day. "I'll never let you down, skipper. I'll always do my part. You can rely on me, skipper." At the time I used to wonder why he would say those things, but never really gave it much thought. We were all young kids busy trying to get some fun out of living and trying not to dwell on the raids. We were all frightened, although no one mentioned it. We might fear the future but we were all in the same boat and there wasn't anything we could do about it.

Fortunately, the raid on Hamburg was our last in Halifax bombers. Number 408 squadron moved from Leeming to Linton, about ten miles from the city of York. There we joined 426 squadron with whom we would share the base, and here we received shiny new Lancaster bombers.

Learning to fly the Lancaster gave our crew a chance to come closer together. We practised bombing, gunnery, and generally learned how to handle the aircraft. It also gave us free hours most evenings and a chance to shoot the breeze with the groundcrews.

Flying Officer Ray Butchart now joined our crew as wireless operator. Ray fitted in beautifully. He was twenty-one and came from Wiarton, Ontario. It was fortunate that his arrival on the squadron coincided with our conversion to the Lanc. Not only did we have time to get acquainted, but more importantly, we could train as a full crew. Converting to the Lanc also brought us into direct contact with more of those instant experts from the Canadian flying schools; those delightful ex-flying instructors.

One such wonder was a Flight Lieutenant whom we had first met at a debriefing following the last raid on Hamburg. Tired, wrung out, and bedraggled I had been standing with a group of other pilots, waiting our turn for debriefing by the intelligence officer. We were drinking large mugs of hot cocoa and standing in front of the huge target maps, covering one wall. Our group was exchanging experiences of the night fighters, flak, searchlights, and the horrible weather, when a Flight Lieutenant joined us and took over the conversation.

He began explaining how the target had been bombed from the wrong direction. "If I had chosen the bomb run," he said, "I'd have set it north to south." Someone challenged his theory and a heated discussion followed. I asked him how many raids he had made. "Oh, I haven't made any yet, I'm just over from Canada." We all turned away in disgust. Yet it was this same guy who was put in charge of training our flight, when we began training on the Lancaster.

One nice summer day, he ordered me and a guy called Mill to the dispersal area, where he was going to show us how the Lancaster worked. He climbed into the pilot's seat and started the engines while Mill and I stood alongside in the aisle. With the engines idling he began running through the tits and taps, explaining the various gauges and controls. "Now," he said, "there are two red wooden handles down here on the floor, on the left side of the pilot's seat." Mill and I couldn't see them. "One," he continued, "is for hot air, and the other, right beside it, is for jettisoning fuel. In an emergency you might have to lighten your bomber and in that case you can dump some gas. When you turn the handle a large horse cock will drop from each wing and the gas will jettison quickly. But," he warned, "don't touch the handle unless you have to. Anyhow, you can't make a mistake because it's wired in the off position with a piece of copper wire. Now the other red handle controls the hot air. In case the engines ice up, you can use this control to give them a burst of hot air, simply by turning the handle. I'll turn it on and you'll notice the boost drop on the manifold gauges."

He reached down to his left and struggled with a handle. We two stared at the engine instruments. Nothing happened. The boost didn't drop. Then the dispersal area turned into a screaming frenzy as the groundcrew yelled to shut off the gas jettison cock. The pad was covered in gas as the two opened gas cocks poured hundreds of gallons onto the ground.

The Flight Lieutenant became an "in joke" among the sergeant aircrews who suffered his constant ideas of how they should train. He was always harassing us to do dinghy or parachute drills his way. He had theories on everything from harmonizing the guns to loading the bombs. I didn't think he knew his ass from a hole in the ground and often told him so. But with his rank he had the authority to order us around.

As we finished our Lanc conversion the day grew near when we would start back on operations. Everyone was anxious to begin, if only to try our new birds in action. The Flight Lieutenant was the keenest of all, or so it seemed. This would be his first operational trip with his own crew and he was going to be prepared.

The magic morning finally arrived and we were awakened with the stomach turning words, "You're on, tonight." When I reached the airfield I was disturbed to find my aircraft S Sugar unserviceable. I was assigned to fly C Charlie. Always totally superstitious I considered this an ill fated omen. As we gathered in the flight rooms that morning the whole squadron was humming, everyone keyed up and busy with last minute preparations. It had been six weeks since we had flown on a raid and everyone was nervous and busy.

No one was busier than the Flight Lieutenant. He was everywhere, harassing his crew, harassing the groundcrew, demanding a new parachute, new flying clothing, a new headset. Back and forth he went to the dispersal to check his Lancaster. His crew were marched along with him. We all felt sorry for his crew and what they endured. Whenever they went flying the Flight Lieutenant would line them up at the rear door, where they were required to salute him as he climbed in first.

Briefing for the night's operation was set for 1500 hours. There we would find out the target, which had been a major matter of concern and discussion. As we entered the briefing room we could see the red ribbon which marked our route, running across the huge wall map of Europe to Stuttgart. Excited babbling arose as everyone found something to say about Stuttgart and how tough it could be. Finally, the CO demanded order and the room hushed. He turned to his adjutant and asked him to call the roll. All present except the Flight Lieutenant and his crew.

"Where in hell are they?" he shouted at the adjutant.

"They wanted to do an air test, sir."

"For Christ's sake, why?" demanded the CO.

Just then the door at the rear of the room flew open and the adjutant said, "Here they come now, sir." All crews turned towards the door to see the Flight Lieutenant striding through, leading his crew and saying, "Sorry we're late, sir." He got halfway up the room, in search of a front seat, when his eyes found the red ribbon leading to Stuttgart. He stopped. Stared. Uttered a small groan and sank backwards onto the floor in a faint.

I think this was the only time I ever heard laughter at an operational briefing. Two officers grabbed his legs and arms and carried him out. We never saw him again. As punishment he was shipped home to Canada. Had he been a sergeant he would have gone to the detention centre.

The sergeant aircrew found a way to make a joke out of the incident. Whenever one of us made a boob the rest would chant, "If you're not more careful, mate, we'll send you home to Canada."

Autopilots Don't Fly

The day the squadron resumed operations was a particularly dramatic and fateful day for our crew.

After the Flight Lieutenant had been carried out and things settled down, the briefing for the raid on Stuttgart began. The CO spoke first, pointing out the target and its importance to the German war effort. He described the types of bombs we would carry, always designed to create the greatest damage for that particular target. He went over the gas loads and the special tactics for our route. He ended by encouraging everyone to do his best and wished us all a good trip.

The intelligence officer followed the CO at the lectern. He detailed the fighter bases near our route, the flak gun emplacements, searchlight batteries, and whatever secret information our intelligence spies had filtered back to England. Next he read out the colours of the day so we could select the various coloured flares we used for identification purposes if challenged by Allied forces. He ended his part of the briefing with the customary caution of maintaining radio silence throughout the trip.

Flying Control then gave marshalling instructions for the aircraft, with takeoff times and home field conditions. Winds and altimeter settings and a time check were rattled off quickly.

The weather briefing followed. This was eagerly awaited by all crews for the inane nonsense and tension relief it provided. It should have been the most important part of the briefing, but in all our weather briefings I never heard one that was coherent. They usually went like this: "You will encounter some cloud over the North Sea, but there may be more than that. Some icing may occur in cloud, but could get heavier. Winds may be strong if you get clear of cloud, but may lessen if the cloud persists, but you may be clear of cloud."

The jibberish of the Met man, universally known as "Cloudy Joe," would keep us smiling as the briefing ended and we broke into groups. The navigators gathered around a huge table with their maps to work out courses, winds, and compass headings for each particular leg of the track. Bomb aimers ran through their bomb loads, and checked the types of markers the Pathfinders would use over the target as the bomb aiming points. The Pathfinders dropped either ground markers, or if the clouds were too thick, parachute flares, that hung in the sky and served as aiming points. This was the least useful method since the wind could drift them off the target. On each raid the colours of the flares were changed in an attempt to fool the Germans, who had begun exploding false target indicators to draw our bombers away from the real objective. They had little effect, for the real target would be a mass of flames shortly after the attack began and there was no mistaking the searchlights and flak streaming up at you.

The time following the briefing was the worst part of bomber operations. Waiting for takeoff. Every aircrew hated and feared the endless hours between briefing and actually taking off. Usually a meal was served a few hours prior to takeoff and we called this the "last supper." It was the only time bacon and eggs – real eggs – were served. They took your mind off the horrors that lay ahead. But only those flying operations that night were served this treat. The rest of the personnel had the usual fried or boiled brussels sprouts, mutton, and potatoes.

Many trips were "scrubbed" at the last moment because of bad weather, and the signal for cancelling the trip was a white flare fired from the control tower. As you waited at your aircraft, standing or sitting on the grass, your eyes strayed furtively and continuously in the direction of the tower. If the weather was foggy or rainy, it added to the apprehension. Of all the separate parts of operational flying – takeoff, outward journey, flying over enemy territory, on the bomb run, enemy attacks, searchlights, flak, or the ordeal of trying to land through fog – the toughest part was waiting. Everyone secretly hoped for a white flare.

As our crew sat that evening on the grass waiting for the time to board the aircraft, we talked about the differences we might find doing operations in the Lancaster. Our conversion from the

Halifax had introduced new techniques and eliminated some old practices. Perhaps the strangest change was the absence of our pigeon, which we had always carried in the Halifax. Waiting to board, I suddenly missed the pigeon and the quiet cooing that always came from his small cage. It was the wireless operator who was responsible for bringing the bird on board, and his job to see it got into the dinghy if the bomber ditched in the sea. If he had time, the wireless operator sent out an SOS from his wireless set, but often there wasn't time, or the radio had been shot away. The pigeon then became the only way to get a message back to base.

The navigator wrote out the aircraft's position in terms of latitude and longitude on a small piece of rice paper. The wireless operator then folded this into the tiny canister attached to the pigeon's leg. When released, the homing pigeon flew off to its roost. There the pigeon master retrieved the message and set the search and rescue operation going.

The practice had grown up in the days of poor radio communications; and the use of pigeons in Canada dated back to 1922, when the RCAF was called the Canadian Air Force. At the end of the war the RCAF had thirty pigeon lofts divided between the east and west coasts of Canada and over 100 airmen trained to look after the flock.

We never thought of the pigeon except for those times when we were waiting to climb aboard for a flight; and once we got underway we seldom remembered it until the next raid. Occasionally, we would speculate on what happened to the bird when we flew above 10,000 feet. The crew turned on oxygen at that height but the poor pigeon didn't have an oxygen mask and simply flopped over in his cage, unconscious. He stayed that way until we arrived back over England and descended.

Our new Lancaster came equipped with a portable radio that was part of the large dinghy stowed in the starboard wing. While the crew bobbed about in the dinghy they could handcrank the portable radio and thus send out an SOS. We had all been trained to crank this monstrosity to produce the required electricity, but it took so much effort that no one liked it. Now, apparently, there was little choice, for the pigeons were declared redundant and officially retired from the squadron. (If you ordered chicken in a restaurant you knew it was pigeon that was served, and a question often flicked across my mind: was a fellow crew member now making the supreme sacrifice?)

The tension of waiting to fly was obvious in everyone and suiting up in the crew room gave a clear indication of the stress everyone felt. I think most aircrew were superstitious. I know I was. We dressed in the same order for each trip. The right flight boot must be put on first. The same heavy socks must be used. Personal pieces of clothing, like a girlfriend's scarf, must be carried. A rabbit's foot or a stuffed toy would be pushed into pockets. Each had his own talisman. Mine was a hockey sweater that I had worn playing for a Toronto team. I wouldn't fly without it. I still have it today and my children wonder why I keep this ragged thing around.

Most crews had a ritual of things they did while standing around the aircraft waiting. Many urinated on the tail wheel for good luck. Others chainsmoked. Some checked the bricks and bottles they would throw out over Germany as their individual contribution to Hitler's woes. Bottles were supposed to make a screaming noise as they fell, and so scare the hell out of the Germans below. Some of the stones had been sent by fathers in food parcels as personal additions to the cause. Occasionally, men vomited before boarding. Eric, our navigator, was one of those. An extremely nervous kid, his hands shook so much you wondered how he could hold a pencil and draw a straight line. He always did. He was one of the sharpest navigators on the squadron.

It was the imaginative types who always had the worst time. They could project the disasters that lay ahead, and had to repeatedly boost their courage. But the strain existed for everyone – even as you climbed aboard and the door slammed behind you. Only when the engines were running, and each member had settled into his crew position and ran through his individual checks, did the tension begin to ease. Radio checks on the crew intercom created a solid, comradely feeling, a togetherness.

This particular night, I had things to think about; and sitting in the dark, with the Lanc throbbing with life, I had time to reflect. This trip was different. It had been six weeks since our last raid and that had been in a Halifax bomber. How would the Lanc perform? These new Lancasters were Mark II's; (only 300 were ever built). Fitted with radial engines, instead of Rolls-Royce in-line engines, they couldn't fly as high as the normal Lanc, although they were faster near the ground and far superior for takeoff. I wondered how high we would actually be able to climb. With a maximum fuel and bomb load it was necessary to climb continuously to some targets to reach 20,000 feet. That height put you above the light flak's effective range but there was still the heavy flak at any height. The secret, I had discovered, in bombing and getting home, was the height you could reach over the target. The higher the better.

I waved the wheel chocks away as soon as I noticed the first Lanc pull out of dispersal, and I followed his bobbing navigation lights along the narrow perimeter track as it trundled to the end of the runway. Keeping the aircraft on the narrow strip was difficult in the dark, and there was the danger of going off into the mud. I steered by goosing the outer engines and using my air brake lever on the control column to check speed as I rounded the bends. Perhaps the worst feature of our heavy bombers was the air brake. The air was fed from a 300 pound pressure tank, which was energized by the starboard inner engine. You ran out of air quickly unless you could rev up that engine and replenish the supply. But revving up the engine gave you too much speed and made you use more brake, which used up the air. The Yanks had hydraulic brakes and we were envious.

I lined up on the runway as our turn came to take off, watching the preceding Lanc thunder down the long runway before lifting. Only his navigation lights were visible, but his slipstream came rolling back to rock our Lanc. Beside me, on the left edge of the runway, I could make out the control van that would give me a "green" from its aldis lamp, which meant "clear to takeoff." Dim figures stood alongside waving. The groundcrew showed up night after night, often standing in the rain to cheer the aircrews on.

A last minute check with each crew member. Everyone set. Harry sat on the jump seat next to me, ready to assist with the throttles on takeoff. Steve, the bomb aimer, had decided to be in his nose position. Normally he stood behind the flight engineer, going forward when we were airborne. Brakes locked on, I eased the four throttles slowly but firmly forward. Harry followed them with his hand to ensure they didn't slip back. Now C Charlie was straining against its brakes. A quick check around the cockpit. Hydraulics, trim, mixture, pitch, centre gas tanks on, flaps twenty degrees, bomb doors closed, windows shut, throttle tension up, directional indicator set on the runway heading. Here we go.

Lead with the two right throttles to counter the powerful torque that could swing you to the right. Release brakes as the engines overpower them. Stick forward to get the tail up quickly and allow the rudder to give direction. Full left rudder to hold her straight as the engines scream into a crescendo. Throttles through the gate and 3,000 revs per engine.

Slowly, the 65,000 pounds began to pick up speed. Swollen with 7,000 pounds of bombs and 2,154 gallons of fuel, the Lanc was slightly over its all up weight. The runway lights came faster, the tail was up and we were going straight as an arrow. Airspeed 90. Airspeed 100. Airspeed 105. The end of the runway leaped towards me. I eased back on the control column, using elevator trim to make a smooth, gradual liftoff.

Back came the stick. Nothing happened. Full up elevator trim, plus nine. Pull harder. Nothing. No response. "Harry, for Christ's sake help, it won't lift off!" Harry jumped off his seat and grabbed the control column with me. We both pulled. We were now off the runway, the lights gone behind, the Lanc bumping over the rough ground. Pitch black. Trees coming up.

"Harder, Harry. Pull, for God's sake, pull!" Suddenly the Lanc reared up, almost straight up, our speed falling to eighty-five knots and towards a stall. "Push, Harry. Down!" I screamed. I rammed the stick forward. Full elevator trim forward. Down went the Lanc and we started a dive. "Pull, Harry. Pull back, we're going down!" Up came the nose, violently. The Lanc rearing vertically. "Push, Harry. Quick, man, get the wheels up!"

Now we had reached 100 feet but the Lanc was going crazy, rolling violently from side to side, trying to roll over and dive. The control column lashed back and forth.

"Someone check the control rods," I yelled at the crew. "They may be jammed!" I checked the automatic pilot but the clutch was out. Carefully, I began raising the flaps.

"Get ready to bale out. I can't keep her flying," I ordered the crew. Slowly, rolling, plunging, climbing, and diving, I struggled up to 5,000 feet. "Everyone call before leaving. Bale out! Bale out!"

Steve wrenched up the escape hatch in the floor of the nose section, but in his haste it jammed and he couldn't get it open. Harry went forward to help. Then a roaring wind told me the hatch was free. I yelled at Harry to hand me my parachute pack. Harry grabbed my chute from its metal holder and clipped it onto the two hooks of my parachute harness. The Lanc was now almost impossible to hold and I strained to keep it level while the crew baled out.

Stan had turned his rear turret sideways, opened the doors behind him, and fallen out backwards. Steve, Harry, and Eric dived through the front escape hatch. Ray and Ken jumped from the back door. Either they called me when they were leaving and I was too panicky to hear them or they dived out without saying they were going. Trapped in my seat, blackness everywhere, I sat there alone, calling each crew member. Silence. They must have baled out. Time for me to go.

Slowly I tried easing out of my seat, but I had forgotten to undo my seat harness. I undid my oxygen hose, unplugged my headset, and pulled the pin on my shoulder harness, grabbing back and forth with one hand, while trying to hold the control column which was still lashing from side to side. Finally, I slid free from the seat and nearer the blast of air coming from the open hatch. As I tried to ease past the throttles, the rip cord of my parachute caught on the throttle levers. Harry, in his haste, had strapped my parachute on with the rip cord on the left side. I was moving to my right. As I slipped into the aisle, still holding the control column, the chute pulled. Parachute silk was everywhere, caught in the blast of air from the open hatch, now hitting me full on. The Lanc reared and began a roll to starboard as I released the control column and clawed at the silk now covering my head.

As the Lanc rolled over and I gathered the silk in my arms, I saw a strut ahead and below in the nose. I reached forward with one hand, clutching at the parachute silk with the other, and pulled myself in a dive towards the open hatch. "This bloody chute won't work now," I thought. Then I was through the hatch and free. *Snap.* One godawful snap, and I knew the chute had worked as my crotch burned from the loose leg straps of my parachute harness. But after that there was nothing. Blackness. Silence. No sensation of falling. No up, no down. No ground, no sky. I felt like I was going up and I cursed the luck that gave me a chute that worked in reverse.

Then *Bang!* The sky came ablaze as the fully loaded Lanc

smashed into the ground below, the bombs and flares lighting up the Yorkshire moors. Then there was blackness again and silence, except for the swish of the air around the parachute. It was a very dark, windy night and I knew I was oscillating wildly. Training manuals and indoor parachute drills had taught me how to control a parachute by pulling on the risers that connected the chute to the canopy of silk overhead. But they hadn't taught me how to do this in the dark when you couldn't see your direction of movement.

The problem was solved with a sudden smash. I landed in a ploughed field on the side of my face. As the chute had pulled me from side to side, I had finally swung up almost level with the canopy – just as the ground rose up to meet me. The silk collapsed for want of air and I fell unassisted.

Dazed, I struggled up from the ground and released the parachute harness, gathering in the silk that was dragging me off balance. I bumped into something hard to find it was a stone wall. Dumping my chute I decided to follow the wall to somewhere. The wall led to a huge stone farmhouse and I groped in the dark night towards the door. Each aircrew member had, as part of his survival gear, a whistle attached to the collar of his battledress. I began blowing my whistle and banging on the farmhouse door. When I thought it would never open, it finally shifted a crack and the light from inside outlined three heads peering out at me. I explained who I was and what had happened and the door slammed shut. Bewildered, I stood there in the dark.

After an eternity the door finally reopened and a huge farmer came out to escort me to the local village about half a mile away. The whole farming area had been awakened by the exploding Lanc and a crowd gathered as we entered the village and the farmer led me to the local constable's house. He wasn't home, but a very pleasant lady, introduced to me as the constable's wife, immediately offered me a cup of tea, and then set about bathing the cuts on my face and hands caused by the buckles on the parachute harness.

As I sat there, the door flew open and the constable rushed in shouting, "They've killed old Tom!" My stomach flipped. Concerned only with my own safety, I hadn't thought about the Lanc exploding. I was sitting behind the door out of sight of the constable drinking my tea, and it was only after his wife had looked in my direction that he turned and saw me. He explained that a local farmer, a friend and a very old man, had rushed out of his farmhouse when he heard the Lanc roaring down. He had been blown back inside his house and killed when the Lanc exploded. I felt sick and helpless. Would this bloody night never end?

The Yorkshire couple were wonderful to me and did their best to reassure me it was all an accident. They phoned the base and had a car sent out. Their thick Yorkshire accents were too much for my tired brain and despite asking to the point of embarrassment, I don't to this day know their names.

I arrived back at base to discover all the crew had made it safely to earth, although Stan had landed in a tree. After a while of hanging by his straps he could feel apples, and decided he couldn't be too high off the ground if it were an apple tree. Rather than spend the night in the tree he decided to risk the fall and released his parachute harness. But the tree was leaning over a hill, and he broke his shoulder as he fell into the ravine.

The official investigation into why the aircraft had crashed never revealed the reason. As far as anyone could determine the automatic pilot had also been trying to fly the Lanc, and although the simple control lever was in the out position it had wanted to take over.

Our bale-out convinced Harry he didn't need any more thrills and he quit. Harry was English, and thirty-five years old. His wife and three children in London were under constant air attack, which put an additional strain on him. He was far too old for flying, and really shouldn't have remustered from groundcrew. But he had wanted to try. All of the crew understood his decision to quit, and while we were sorry to lose him, we all agreed it was the wise thing to do.

Have Lanc, Will Play

When the weather was fine for flying in England it was often terrible over the Continent and ops would be postponed. Then we did local flying. Either a "bull's-eye" exercise that put you over English towns at night on a dummy raid, complete with searchlights but no flak, or practice bombing runs, without bombs. During the day we had gunnery practice, fighter practice against friendly Spitfires, compass swings, or air tests to check various pieces of equipment. The best of all was local flying practice.

Those were the times that presented an opportunity for low flying, which was strictly forbidden. But over the Yorkshire moors or over the North Sea, who was to know? It was the pilot's only chance to really throw the Lanc all over the sky and discover just what a beautiful machine he had. The Lanc looked right just sitting on the tarmac, and as any pilot knows (and to echo R. J. Mitchell, the designer of the Spitfire), "If it looks right, it usually is."

Faster than the early Halifax or B-17 Fortress, the Lancaster was a most forgiving kite. It stalled normally and gently, straight ahead, with no tendency to drop a wing. You could land it nicely from 100 to 130 miles an hour, depending on whether you wanted to three-point the landing or wheel it onto the runway. The cockpit visibility was the best of any bomber and it responded to the controls with a light touch. No vices and not a thing to worry about. It was essentially a flying bomb bay, and could carry double the bomb load of the Halifax or Fortress and carry it farther.

Later versions, with more powerful engines and strengthened fuselages, were adapted to carry a 22,000 pound bomb: the largest bomb ever carried by any aircraft. Its bomb bay was refigured and lengthened and the doors removed to accommodate this

Grand Slam bomb. These monsters were used late in the war against the German submarine pens hidden below thirty feet of reinforced concrete.

The Lanc could easily fly on two engines, and some crews made it home on one engine, using a shallow dive over the last few miles. For a lark, I once feathered all four engines while practise flying at 5,000 feet. The silence was beautiful as the four engines ceased their tremendous roaring. I glided down, losing only 800 feet a minute, the Lanc still responsive and light on the controls. It made me wish for a sound-proof cockpit. With the engines stopped, the crew were able to chat away without using the intercom.

The Lancaster did not emerge full blown from the factory, as did some wartime aircraft. It really started as a two-engined thing called the Manchester and named after the town where it was born. The A. V. Roe Company had flown the first prototype in July 1939, but soon discovered its two Vulture engines were underpowered. They went back to the drawing board and redesigned the entire aircraft, replacing the two Vulture engines with four Rolls-Royce Merlins and adding a central fin between the two small outboard fins. It was then early 1941, and the design still did not suit Roy Chadwick, the chief designer. Back to the drawing board. In the early spring the final design was fixed and the Lancaster, with four Merlins and its distinctive twin tail, went into production. The first Lancaster flew on operations in 1942.

Each machine cost about $200,000 and each contained over 50,000 separate parts which were manufactured in various aircraft factories around England. Each factory contributed a specific section to a central assembly plant at Chadderton.

Separate production was started in Canada by Victory aircraft in 1942, and this plant produced over 400 Mark X Lancs. The first one was flown to England by Reggie Lane, who had distinguished himself flying with the Pathfinders. He arrived at Linton with the brand new Lanc, named the "Ruhr Express." We all poked around it, but except for its Packard-Merlin engines it looked just like our Mark II models.

It was thought the Lancaster couldn't take as much punishment as the Halifax but that was difficult to believe. Lancs came home riddled with holes, with turrets blown away, fins missing, aerials or ailerons shot off, windscreens and noses destroyed, hydraulic lines severed, radios dead, tires blown, flaps ripped apart, wheels hanging down, propellers missing, engines torn away, control rods smashed, wing tips crumpled or missing or wings themselves punctured by bombs falling through from planes flying above. Lancs came limping home hours late, to crash, slithering and sliding, dirt and grass flying, propellers churning the ground. Some burst into flames. Some had dead or wounded crew slumped in smoke-blackened turrets. But home they came, time after time, when it was impossible to believe they could remain in the air. To say the crews loved the Lancaster is to understate the case.

Low flying in the Lanc was exhilarating as you cruised at 230 miles an hour over the farms, hills, and valleys of Yorkshire. A favourite sport was chasing horses, or pulling up over a haywagon and watching the hay blow and the farmers scrambling away. Over the North Sea we would chase seagulls low over the water, the gunners blazing away, but to my knowledge never hitting anything. Firing the two machine guns in the front turret into the sea would cause the spray to come completely over the windscreen. We would often take another pilot along so we could take turns firing ahead from the turret. It was necessary to get down to two or three feet above the water to make the spray come over the cockpit. It made the adrenalin flow.

The crew seemed to enjoy low flying, especially the gunners who would roar with laughter as we ran a horse over a fence or dove on a British anti-aircraft gun battery, scattering the crew. They always rushed for cover. Had they put a few rounds past our ears it might have taught us something. With the exuberance of youth we didn't care for the army who, as far as we were concerned, didn't do anything but march around England. We were fighting the war and didn't mind telling them so.

One nice summer day, we were low flying, just horsing around over the Yorkshire moors. We had taken off to do gunnery practice over the sea, which was only twenty minutes from base. We usually went out over the coastal town of Scarborough as low as possible. Now, on our return to base, I again pushed the nose down and started skimming the hills and plunging into the valleys. The crew chattered away, pointing out things to "shoot up." I found a red-tiled roof on a farmhouse which was standing on a hill, and pushing the nose down farther, I aimed just below the roof line. I wondered if I could blow some tiles off with the slipstream if I pulled up at the right moment. With the throttles wide open I roared at the house, then at the last moment I heaved back on the stick and went straight up. Several of the tiles flew off the roof and the crew laughed and hooted, describing the scene for me. Now I really got into the mood and down I went into a flat valley where farmers were cutting hay and forking it onto wagons.

Zoom, right over the wagons. The hay flew and the horses bolted. Chuckling with glee, my head turned to watch, I didn't see the shadow ahead. *Crash!* I flew right through the top of a huge, luckily dead, tree. The windscreen in front of Jock disintegrated with a bang as a bird came smashing through, hitting him in the face. I turned to look, and horrified, saw that his face was streaming with blood. My God, I've killed him! Eric ran forward with the first aid kit and began swabbing the blood from Jock's face. Only then did we realize it was the bird's blood and not Jock's. The rush of air coming through the smashed windscreen was blowing bits of bird and a swirl of feathers down the inside of the aircraft.

Blinded by the slipstream blasting in I pulled my goggles over my eyes and, thoroughly chastened, climbed up to a safer altitude. I checked the instruments to find the two starboard engines overheating. I feathered both engines and turned for base. How to explain the damage? As I settled the Lanc into a two-engined approach for landing and began rounding out, I noticed some bushes just off the end of the runway. They stood about four feet high. Ha.

Shutting down at dispersal I could see that the engineering officer had gathered with some groundcrew and as the two engines died, I could hear them talking and pointing. Climbing out I joined them as they stood under the wing, pulling sticks and branches from the oil coolers, which hung beneath the Hercules engines. "What happened?" asked the engineering officer. I turned towards the end of the runway, pointed, and said in as stern a voice as I could muster, "Those bloody trees off the end of the runway. I've asked you guys a hundred times to cut them down. I flew right through them." They bought it.

Without a grumble the groundcrew got busy and replaced the windscreen and oil coolers, and we flew on ops that night.

Intrepid Birdmen

Tiny Ferris, who hailed from Calgary, was the CO of 408 squadron when I joined it in June 1943. Tiny was something else; a rough, tough, former bush pilot who didn't know the word fear. The squadron thought he was the greatest and so did I – despite our disagreement over a captain's responsibility. His navigator, however, didn't always think he was so great.

The CO's crew was composed of the various leaders on the squadron. The navigation leader, the gunnery leader, the bombing leader and so on. Ferris' navigator was a long suffering Flight Lieutenant who often threatened to fly with another crew. It seemed Ferris didn't pay too much attention to the courses laboriously worked out by his navigator, who remained continually frustrated in his attempts to keep the aircraft on track and on time.

Ferris loved to take new pilots on their first operational trips. He would attempt to show the sprog pilot the dangers of straying off course and over defended areas by deliberately heading the bomber off track over a city. The place would come alive with lights and shells. The crew would be scared out of their wits and the new pilot certain he wasn't going to like operational flying. Ferris, oblivious to their fears, would weave around in the flak and searchlights before heading off the city. Naturally, this threw the navigator's plot into disarray and him into a frenzy. As the squadron navigation leader he should have the best navigational plot, not the worst, and he knew the other navigators would check his log the next day and smirk.

One pilot, returning bewildered from his first raid as "second dickie" to Ferris, told me about his experiences. The route that night had passed close to Hanover, just a few miles north. As they were passing Hanover, Ferris, deciding to show the sprog some action, did a ninety degree turn south and flew over the city. The whole earth opened up and the plane got some holes before getting off the city and back north. Ferris turned to the pilot and said, "Now don't you ever do that." Then he called the navigator and asked what course he was supposed to fly. The navigator was beside himself with fury. He shouted at Ferris, "There are 360 fucking degrees on your compass. Pick any one you want. I've finished navigating!"

Ferris, as I said, was something else. He was one of the few officers on our base who would give the time of day to non-commissioned (NCO) aircrew. When he had finished his tour of ops he was posted to an administration job. Before he left the squadron his adjutant gathered the entire squadron in the hangar for a farewell salute. He didn't tell Ferris it was a farewell, he told him it was a mutiny. All crews were refusing to fly and were going on strike.

When Ferris received the phone call, he jumped into his staff car and raced to the hangar where we were all assembled. He screeched to a stop and literally dove out the car door. Running up to his adjutant, who was standing in front of the entire squadron, he screamed, "What the hell's going on here?"

The adjutant stuck the mug of beer he had been hiding behind his back into Ferris' face and the squadron broke into "So drink, Chug A Lug," the song used at all farewells:

Here's to Ferris, he's true blue.
He's a drunkard, through and through.
So drink, chug a lug, chug a lug, chug a lug,
So drink, chug a lug, chug a lug, chug a lug.

The lines were repeated until the tankard had been drained and placed upside down on Ferris' head. Then three mighty cheers and a tiger rang out. Ferris could normally knock off a pint at one draught, but this time he had trouble. The surprise had been so cleverly conceived and concealed.

Ferris had a favourite saying: "Screwed, blued, and tattooed." When a crew arrived back from leave they got that one. "Well, I suppose now that you guys have all been screwed, blued, and tattoed, you're ready for some ops." I understood the first and last words but had trouble with the word blued and had to have it explained. The reference was to the blue ointment the doctors used to cure a case of body crabs attacking the pubic area.

Our world was filled with pseudonyms, acronyms, code names, slang expressions, and monikers. A party was a *knees up,* a *bash,* or a *do,* with everyone getting *screechers.* It was more fun than bingo, or *housie-housie.* Tea was *char* or *tiffen,* and the biscuit you ate with the tea was a *wad.* Sausages were *bangers.* Candies were *sweets* or *horlicks.* A cigarette was a *nail,* a *fag,* a *Lucifer,* a *gasper,* a *wild Woodbine,* or a *Senior Service.*

Money was *ackers* or *lolly* or *gilt,* and was expressed in *guineas, quids, pounds,* or *shillings.* You took it when you went to London, the *Big Smoke,* to look for girls who were *skirts, popsies, queens, sheilas, birds, crumpets,* or *fluff.* In the city you might go to the movies, which were *flicks* you saw at the *cinema* – and you probably had to get in a lineup or *queue* for them.

Across the Channel, Berlin was the *Big City* or the *Holy City.* The Ruhr Valley was *Happy Valley,* and Hitler was *Adolf.* The King was *George* – and anything of greatness was thus *real George.* On the other hand, a fiasco was an *absolute shower,* a *fuck up,* or a *proper balls up;* and if it was your fault you could be *bollocksed* or *rumbled.* You had your *finger in* or your *finger up* and were encouraged to get your *finger out.*

Germans were *Huns* or *Jerries,* while prisoners of war were *kriegees* or *gefangeners.* Every other nationality seemed to have a slang name as well. The Scots were called *Jock;* the Irish, *Paddy;* the Welsh, *Taffy.* The English were *Limeys, broncos, pommies,* or *kippers.* Australians were *Aussies*; Americans, *Yanks*; Frenchmen, *Frogs*; Italians, *Eye-ties;* New Zealanders, *Kiwis;* and Arabs *A-rabs* or *wogs.* Canadians were just Canadians – unless they were those Bloody Canadians!

The different positions and services also had their own names. Instrument technicians were *instrument bashers.* Groundcrew were *erks* or *plonks* or *fitters* or *riggers.* Supply types were *bin rats.* Service police were *narks* or *square heads* or *meat heads.* The CO was the *old man* or the *groupie* or the *wingco;* and the senior warrant officer was *sergeant-major* or *major.* The intelligence officer was a *gen merchant;* (information was *gen,* and misleading information *duff gen*). A research scientist was a *boffin* or *backroom*

boy. Nurses were *nursing machines.* The air force itself consisted
of *Brylcreem boys* or *pigeons,* and in it all new crews were *sprogs.*
The head of the airwomen was the *Queen Bee,* and her girls were
WAAF's. Soldiers were *Tommies* or *wallahs, ground pounders* or
pongos, GI's or *grunts.* Sailors were *salts* or *matelots* or *nautics,*
and all of them were considered to be like Lord Nelson: *one eye,*
one arm, one asshole. Nearly everyone had a moniker like Spike,
Flash, Longfellow, Tinkle, Sea-level, Rope, Mush, or Shoe.

The actual aircraft had affectionate names, too. The Wellington
was *Wimpey;* the Spitfire, *Spit;* the Lancaster, *Lanc;* the Hampden, *Cigar.* The Halifax was a *Hally Bag;* Typhoons were *Tiffies;*
and Hurricanes were *Hurrys.* They were all *kites* or *crates* or *birds,*
flown by *peelots* or *captains* or *skippers* or *jockeys* or *drivers.* The
cockpit was the *greenhouse* or *front office,* and all instruments
there were *tits* or *taps* or *clocks* – except for the needle and ball,
which was the *knife and fork.* The control column was the *stick* or
pole or *yoke.* The landing wheels were the *gear* or the *landing cart.*
Brakes were *anchors* or *binders.* An engine was a *donk,* and to
stop an engine in the air was to *feather the prop.* A radio was a
wireless, and wireless operators were *wops* or *wags* or *sparks. Gee*
was the first radar navigation aid, and navigators were *alligators.*
The rear-gunner was *tail-end Charlie.*

To be told to *get some in* meant to do some operational flying.
Sometimes the raid was a *good show,* a *wizard prang,* or a *grand*
party. Did you bomb the target? *Bang on.* How was your trip? *A*
piece of cake. On other occasions, the operation didn't go well. It
was a *shaky do* or a *hairy do* or a *snafu: situation normal all*
fucked up. Maybe you failed to complete the operation and
aborted the trip. Then you had an *early return* and wrote *DNCO* in
the log. Maybe the aircraft was *duff* or *ropey* – it didn't fly properly – and you had to crash, or *prang,* and *write off* the plane.
When flying over water you used a life preserver called a *Mae West*
in case you fell in the *drink* and had to *ditch.* To use a parachute
was to *hit the silk* or *pull the handle* or *bale out,* and to send an
SOS was to call *DARKY.* To panic meant to *flap* or go into a *flat*
spin. If, in consequence, you were called to the CO's office, you
were *on the carpet* receiving a *rocket* or *blast* and being
shit on from a great height. To receive military punishment was to
get *jankers* and thrown in the *quod.* Crews who didn't return from
ops had *bought the farm, gone for a burton, got the chop,* or *gone*

for a shit. If, however, you completed your tour you were *screened*. And to retire from the air force was to receive your *bowler*.

Meanwhile, there was flying. Low level operations were *rhubarbs*, and at 10,000 feet you were *Angels 10*. Droning to the target was *stooging*. A quick turn was a *split-ass turn*; a loose flying formation a *gaggle*. To fly at full throttle was to have your *balls to the wall* or to be *flat out* – and when you did that you were *haring over the deck*. To fly down a railway track was to fly on the *iron compass*, but you usually read a map and looked for a *pinpoint* to get a *fix* to correct your *heading* and *ETA*. After all this, to land an aircraft was to *pancake*!

A drizzle was *scotch mist*, and if you were on the ground you could wear a *mac* or put up a *brolly*. Bad weather would be *soupy* or *clampers*. To fly in it was to fly in the *clag* on the *clocks*, which was *dicey* and only done by *intrepid birdmen*. When you didn't fly you were *stood down*. You could take the time to sleep – a guy who was sleeping had *hit the sack* or *flaked out* or was in the *wanker* – or you could go to the pubs and fraternize. When you disagreed with someone over the bar you told him to *get stuffed*, or he told you to *belt up*, which meant shut up. A dumb airman was a *clot*, a *clod*, a *moron*, a *sod*, and sometimes a *blighter*. If he was crazy he was *bonkers* or *crackers* and probably had the *twitch*. When there was no chance of *clobbering* a target (or of getting *clobbered* by a German fighter yourself), there could be a parade, a *square bashing*, or a non-flying day, called a *make and mend day*. Then you could review mechanical problems that were caused by *bugs* or *gremlins* and were known as *snags*. Anything was better than paperwork, or *bumft*.

The slang touched almost everything. The RCAF Headquarters was the *head shed*. A medal was a *gong*. The telephone was the *horn*, and using a public phone meant pressing *Button A* and *Button B*. A streetcar was a *tram* or *trolley*, and the conductor a *clippie*. Trucks were *lorries, vans,* or *hundred weights*. Bomb carts were *dollies*. The battery was an *ack*; the gasoline truck a *bowser*; and gas itself was *petrol*. Radar sets were *black boxes*; *OBOE* was the radio beam automatic bombing device; and *H2S* the first, primitive, on-board radar navigation instrument used to locate the target. *Wanganui* were Pathfinder sky markers; *Paramatta* the ground markers. *Scarecrows* were huge flares exploded by the Germans in the bomber stream. Sometimes terms referred to more than one thing. A mechanics wrench was a *spanner* for instance; but golf clubs could also be *spanners*.

Very few of these expressions originated with Canadians, and while the Aussies and the Kiwis did add some colourful terms, the majority were vintage RAF. The years between the wars had given the RAF time to move away from army and navy expressions and develop some of their own. Our talk might sometimes have been confusing to outsiders – but it was certainly never drab.

The Other Half

The guy who replaced Ferris as CO was no bargain – yet another of those ex-flying instructors who had spent too much time on the theory of flight and not enough time thinking about operational flying. Impractical is the only word that describes them. The contrast between Ferris and the new CO was painfully apparent to everyone. He had no time for sergeant aircrew and we rarely caught a glimpse of him. He never paid a visit to our flight rooms or to the sergeants' mess or to our barracks. I doubt he knew any of our names. He was killed six weeks after taking command, only to be replaced by the same type. Training Command types. That was the vilest description any of us could apply to them.

Not long after he assumed command I received a call to report to his office immediately. I had no idea what he wanted, but the timing couldn't have been worse. The built-up resentment which seethed inside me over the "system" and its inequality had reached a boiling point.

I sat in the CO's office while he explained that the RCAF was coming out with a new approach. All NCO pilots and navigators were to be commissioned as officers. He asked me what i thought of that. I went over the stupidity of a system that divided a crew, when the essence of survival was teamwork. Solidarity. Everyone equal in every way. I ended by saying I would be happy to have a commission if the other NCO's in my crew were also offered commissioned rank. The CO said that was impossible. "Do you really think," he asked me, "that air gunners and flight engineers should be officers?"

"Why not?" I replied, "they do the same job that I do." After some heated words, back and forth, I repeated that I wasn't interested in a commission unless all the crew became officers.

"You'll have to sign a waiver to that effect," he said.

"Fine," I replied, "where do I sign?"

The adjutant brought in a form and I signed, refusing a commission to the rank of Pilot Officer. What the hell do I care, I thought. I can't leave Stan and Ken out in that crumby barracks, and we can't go on leave to our old haunts if I'm an officer and they're NCO's. Who needs officer quarters? To hell with the commission.

One other sergeant pilot at Linton, a member of 426 squadron and a French-Canadian, Roger Coulombe, also refused his commission for the same reason I had given. His refusal was couched in better language than mine. Looking his CO straight in the eye, he said in heavily accented English, "You can stick your commission to your arse."

Our decision to reject officer status was not a fight against the rank structure of the RCAF. That was not in question. We understood the need for a structured, orderly organization. What was impossible to grasp was the artificial splitting of a crew by rank and therefore social status, when our lives were totally interdependent. A successful crew was a cohesive unit, each component equal in professionalism, each member respectful of his fellow crew members and of the expertise he contributed to the whole. But the respect started with the man and not the trade. This was the reason the RCAF took time at Operational Training Units to ensure that people had compatible personalities before they were allowed to come together as a flying unit. Commissioning only pilots and navigators wrecked that system. It separated the crews with social barriers, pay differences, and living conditions. Now some were more equal than others.

One night we were hit by a snowstorm an hour before scheduled takeoff. The storm dumped three inches of heavy, wet snow on the base. Since our base hadn't any snow removal equipment it looked doubtful the bombers could get airborne. The aircraft from both squadrons had been marshalled in a line leading to the end of the runway. The CO of my squadron was the first in line for takeoff; Roger Coulombe's Lancaster was next, and mine was third.

All the aircrews, together with the groundcrews, were busy with sticks and brooms trying to get the snow off wings and fuselages.

It was a losing battle since the wet snow clung to everything, and it was difficult to see in the dark. We slipped and skidded high on the wings but accomplished little. Finally, we all gathered at the end of the runway for a conflab. Time was running out. Either we started taking off in a few minutes or we would be late over the target and sitting ducks.

My CO turned to Roger and said, "I'll pull out of line and you move onto the runway. If you make it, we'll all follow."

Roger glared at him. "You are in the number one position. You take off. If you make it, we'll all follow."

The CO yelled to the crowd of airmen, "The trip is scrubbed. Get your aircraft back to your dispersals."

Roger, I thought, had both guts and common sense. He would go on to fly fourteen of the sixteen Berlin raids, a feat no one else accomplished. The episode, however, convinced me, if I needed any convincing, that sergeant aircrew were considered inferior and expendable, if they were considered at all.

It was shortly after this demonstration of leadership that the station received visits from two dignitaries whose philosophies and leadership qualities were so different that their visits are firmly fixed in my mind.

Both squadrons were assembled in a hangar one afternoon. When our crew arrived, the place was packed and we had to stand at the rear. A raised platform had been erected at one end of the hangar and several senior officers were already seated there. Suddenly the crowd hushed, as a portly, very senior officer climbed onto the platform.

It ran through the crowd like the wind. "It's Bomber Harris!" It was indeed. Air Chief Marshal Sir Arthur Harris, Air Officer Commanding-in-Chief, Bomber Command. We were impressed.

Although we didn't know it at the time, we were to learn that this was one of the very few occasions that Harris ever visited a squadron during the course of the war. This was the man who directed the entire bomber offensive. The one man, it seemed, who understood what the war was all about. The same guy we would disparage over our beers as Bomber Harris or Butcher Harris. We would picture him standing in his office, a glass of Scotch in hand, looking out the window at the fog or rain or snow and saying, "It looks fine to me, chaps. Send them off." At the same time we had tremendous respect for him, for it was obvious, even at our level, that he fought very hard to get all the many support services the squadrons required to keep operational. We had heard enough about him to know he was a winner. Harris was introduced by the station commander.

Harris had lived and worked in Rhodesia for a time and still had a certain twang to his speech. It certainly twanged that day. "More than half of you won't be here in a few weeks," was his opening sentence. It got full attention from everyone. Harris continued, "We are about to begin a series of raids that will demand the best from all of you. We know there will be tremendous losses, but it has to be done. You've all done a splendid job, but the real test is still before you. We must beat Germany to her knees." What he was saying, although we didn't know it, was that the Battle of Berlin was about to start. He went on for a few more minutes in a similar vein and then asked for questions. There was complete silence as everyone looked at everyone else. Who wanted to ask this hardbitten bastard anything?

Suddenly, a voice beside me shouted, "How come sergeant air gunners only get $2.25 a day and sergeant pilots and navigators get $3.70 a day and we all do the same job?" I recognized the questioner as a rear gunner from our squadron. Harris couldn't see him and called, "Who said that?"

The gunner yelled back, "I did."

"Come up here," roared Harris.

We all waited, straining forward, as the gunner made his way to the platform. This was going to be good. Old Bomber would probably tear a strip off the poor sergeant. But Harris greeted him warmly and shook hands, before asking him to repeat his question. Then he turned to the crowd and said, "I don't know. It's another one of those damn crazy things that get started and after a while no one knows why. I don't agree with it, but I can't change it."

The direct, honest way Harris had answered brought a roar of respect from the crowd, and he went down in our books as a man you could trust.

A far different gathering took place soon after. Again our crew was late and had to stand at the back of the hangar. We arrived just in time to see a bunch of dignitaries climbing the steps to the platform, led by a short, tubby civilian, wearing a bowler hat. The hangar exploded in a roar of boos. Startled, I turned to ask, "Who is this guy?" Many didn't know but we were booing lustily. Finally a groundcrew flight sergeant enlightened me.

"It's Mackenzie King," he said.

"Who's he?" I asked.

A look of disdain came over the flight sergeant's face. "Our prime minister, you asshole."

I really hadn't known, nor had half the crowd in that hangar. Yet we all booed vigorously. It took several years before I fully understood how much the Canadian servicemen detested the man and his weak-kneed war policies.

Surviving On The Ground

Living in wartime Britain was always interesting, even when not flying. The strange customs and accents, the weird characters, the blackouts, the fog and constant foul weather, were new and different. They gave us something extra.

Like everyone else, eating or finding something decent to eat was constantly on my mind. The mess cooks tried but they had little with which to work and we were always hungry. Margarine was a recent invention and huge white blocks of it, hard as stone, decorated every table. Often the evening meal was boiled or fried brussels sprouts, potatoes, and some kind of meat, like greasy mutton. Breakfast was more brussels sprouts, reheated from the night before and referred to as ''bubble and squeak,'' or simply a piece of bread soaked in cooking grease and fried. Powdered milk and powdered eggs were, like margarine, ersatz creations that proved necessity the mother of invention. Although they should have been declared inedible, they were wolfed down by starving troops.

One of the unsung British heroes of the war was the Englishman who had developed the new strain of brussels sprouts. His new variety grew profusely and the yields were three or four times greater than the older strains of these tiny cabbages. Every day huge truckloads arrived on base to our raucous cheers. I can't remember a meal without them. God, how we all hated them! They did their part in keeping starvation at bay, but they couldn't have been a worse choice for aircrew required to fly at high altitude in unpressurized aircraft. Modern diets for aircrew call for less volatile ingredients. Luckily we all wore oxygen masks, which filtered out most of the gaseous smells.

Fortunately, most of our food could be camouflaged with table-sauce as only the English make it. Huge bottles sat on every table. Half a quart spilled over the soggy brussels sprouts or canned spam altered the taste considerably. My favourite sauce was named "Daddy's." It came in a tall bottle with a label that read, "The only sauce I dare give Father."

Our crew would journey far afield searching for a café that served something that tasted like food. We found such a spot in the town of Rippon, about fifteen miles from our base. It was owned by a young widow. Her air gunner husband had been killed over Germany. This gal, much to our satisfaction, discriminated.

Seated in the small, permanently crowded café, you were surrounded by army types. The featured item on the menu was bacon and eggs, always a rare treat. If you were in air force uniform your eggs always sat a little higher on your plate. Underneath the two eggs lay a small steak. None of the army guys got this treatment and we felt special.

The Canadian Army had been in England since 1939. They were bored and tired of the constant field exercises, route marches, and guard duty. The murderous assault on Dieppe had been their sole foray and they itched to get into action. The British Army was stationed overseas in Africa, Burma, and other hideous places, while the Canadians looked after England and the English ladies. The soldiers were a rough, tough bunch who called the air force the "Brylcreem boys."

My older brother, Frank, was one of them. Stationed in the south of England with a tank recovery unit of the RCEME, he had been up and down in rank from private to sergeant so many times he had lost count. I would look him up occasionally when I went on leave, and he would let me sit at the controls of his huge recovery truck that could lift a sixty ton disabled tank. It was when I was with him that I learned how other services lived, and it made me less bitchy about my own living conditions.

One night we arranged to meet at the railway station in Red Hill, where we planned to go into London for the evening. Frank was standing on the station platform when I arrived, looking strangely pregnant. I asked what was the matter. He unbuttoned his battle-dress blouse and pulled out a new pair of army boots and a blanket.

"What in hell are you doing with those?" I asked in amazement.

"I need money for beer, don't I?" Anything not nailed down was yours, or so it seemed to him and his army pals.

When Frank came to visit me on the squadron, I would sew sergeant stripes on his sleeve in order to get him into the mess. He enjoyed those visits, especially watching our bombers take off and the excitement of the base during the day of a raid. He thought our sleeping quarters excellent, and couldn't understand my complaints. "You should sleep under a truck in the mud for a few nights," he told me. "That would shut you up."

Every six weeks aircrew flying on bombing operations received nine days leave. God knows who figured out the formula, but we didn't care who, as long as it rolled around. Since my crew was a mixture of officers and non-commissioned officers we never went on leave as a crew. We might fly together but our social life was quite different. I usually went to London for the nine days with Stan and Ken. Eric visited the English girl he was soon to marry, Jock went home to Glasgow, or so he said, and Steve and Ray usually visited relatives.

London was the place. The Big Smoke, as it was called by the troops. Bed and breakfast, two and six: two shillings and sixpence. Since we were sergeant aircrew we didn't have much money. As a pilot I got $3.70 a day and the gunners got $2.25. The uniform was provided, I didn't smoke, and two pints of English beer were a full night.

Like all kids hitting a foreign city we were anxious to explore all of the attractions possible – the Tower of London, Madame Tussaud's Wax Museum, Fleet Street, Baker Street, Threadneedle Street, Hyde Park, Buckingham Palace, the Strand, Piccadilly Circus, Covent Garden, St. Paul's, Trafalgar Square, Whitehall, Houses of Parliament, Bond Street, the Fish Market, the Underground – name it and we gawked at it. We used all the clichés common to the times. Looking at the Tower of London Ken would say, "It would hold a lot of hay, if it was baled." Or, "This place looks bigger than Moosomin." We revelled in the English cabs, trod the bridges and the Embankment, and rode the double-decker buses from the topside.

Nights were spent going from pub to pub, chatting up the WAAF's or WREN's or WAAC's or Land Army Girls. Of all the uniforms worn by the girls, the Land Army Girls' uniform was the hardest to remove. Heavy, dark green turtleneck sweater, tucked into breeches, that were tucked into knee-high boots. We called them the "iron maidens." One of the girls we would see from time to time in London was a WREN. A pretty, dark haired girl, she could outdrink everyone in the pub. As the evening wore on and ideas of taking her home to bed crept into my mind, the inevitable always happened. She would wet her pants.

Arguments occurred as you bumped into Yanks, especially those flying Liberator or Fortress bombers on daylight raids. We thought them crazy to bomb in daylight and accused them of not being able to navigate in the dark. But they were mostly friendly arguments, spiced with a certain envy over the pay they got. As you fingered your shillings at the bar, the Yanks would be folding pound notes. Farther down the bar, the RAF kids were counting sixpences.

Canada badges on your shoulder helped in England, and the Bobbies and civilians always went out of their way to give directions. The only narky ones were the railway station attendants. When you asked them for directions in the blacked out stations, either they didn't know or they wouldn't tell you.

London was constantly under attack. Night after night the anti-aircraft guns would roar and lumps of spent shells rattled down with the bombs. Everyone seemed to take it all in stride. But there were times I wondered why we needed to spend our leave in such a hot spot.

Strolling through Hyde Park one summer afternoon, I fell in behind two elderly ladies who were using walkingsticks. As I was watching them, a buzz bomb roared into sight. These flying bombs made a hideous racket. They were launched from the coast of Europe and targeted for London. You only needed to worry if you heard the rocket motor cut out. As soon as the engine cut, the bomb nosed over and plunged to earth. This one did just that. The two elderly ladies took three steps and dove headfirst under a park bench, skirts and walkingsticks flying. The buzz bomb passed over us and exploded outside the park, shaking the ground I was standing on. With that the two ladies crawled out from under the bench and with a dignity only the English can muster, proceeded sedately on their walk.

Kids continually followed you asking for gum or candy. "Any

gum, chum" became a favourite saying among the aircrews, usually attempted in a mock cockney accent. We always tried to carry a small stock to hand out. For my part it was mostly to hear the piping voices with their strange but attractive accents.

The blackout, especially on foggy nights, added to the excitement and high adventure of exploring London. If you got lost in your wanderings you had the "tube" to take you home. Here, as you walked down the steps to the underground system, you stepped over hundreds of people sleeping on the platforms or the stairs. Londoners had been under air attack for three years and many had been bombed out of their homes. It brought the war a lot closer.

Moving around the city in daylight you saw the huge craters and blasted buildings. There were areas cordoned off by ropes, as crews dug for unexploded bombs. Guards were posted with large signs proclaiming UXB.

A celebrated incident at that time was the story told by Lord Trenchard, father of the RAF, and at this point in his career, head of Scotland Yard. Trenchard used a walkingstick. He was quite a huge, imposing man, nicknamed "Boom" for his voice. A tremendous leader, Trenchard had fought to have a separate air force over the bitter opposition of the navy and army. It was Trenchard who went to King George V and had him personally approve the RAF Ensign, which effectively established the RAF as a separate entity and silenced the navy and army. He was touring the bomb damage with a small party of his police officials one day, and came upon a roped off area with a policeman posted on guard on the far side. Climbing over the ropes, Trenchard started around the edge of the huge crater towards the policeman. When he got up to him he was surprised to hear, "You aren't allowed inside the ropes, sir. There is an unexploded land mine buried down there that could go off at any minute."

"Why then," roared Trenchard, "in God's name, did you allow me over the ropes?"

The policeman said, "Oh, I thought I recognized you, sir."

Sometimes when I needed to get away from uniforms and the military to try and think, I would spend my nine days visiting Aunt Martha instead of going to London. Martha wasn't really my aunt, but a third cousin of my mother's. She lived alone in Bolton, just north of Manchester. Those days spent in her tiny row house, usually in the rain, refreshed me and took away the constant thought of the next raid.

Martha was a diminutive, lively person who had never married. She worked in a textile mill and had done so since she was fourteen. Martha had no immediate family and except for a spinster girlfriend and several aunts was alone in the world. She must have been very attractive when younger and I often wondered why she had never married. I didn't ask and it was only years later when I brought her to France, where I was living, that I learned why.

I had taken mother and Martha on a tour of European battlefields and War Cemeteries. We were standing in the reconstructed trenches of Vimy Ridge and marvelling at how close the trenches were to the German lines. Martha had been busy reading all the plaques and posted information which explained the slaughter called the Battle of Vimy Ridge. She turned to me and said, "None of the young men from our town came back from here."

In her Bolton home, Martha had a budgie bird for a companion that she talked to constantly in her peculiar Lancashire accent. Martha called him Teddy, and would say his name and his address to him by the hour. "Teddy Hulme, 422 Halliwell Road." Teddy had this off by heart and would recite it back in the same accent. He escaped one day while Martha was cleaning his cage. She was frantic and we searched up and down the street looking everywhere. No sign of Teddy. Poor Martha was heartbroken and went about telling the shopkeepers and neighbours to keep their eyes open for him. The next day an old codger showed up at her door holding Teddy in his cap. Martha screamed with delight. It seems the old pensioner had been dozing outside the local pub waiting until it opened. Teddy landed on his head. He quickly reached up and caught the bird. Then, holding Teddy and talking to him, the old fellow had made friends. Teddy had announced his name and address and was promptly delivered, folded carefully in the peaked cap.

Going with Martha to the various vaudeville and stage shows then so prevalent in England was a hilarious experience. Mostly amateur reviews, they made up in spirit what they lacked in polished performances. With Martha roaring with laughter and rattling her candy wrappers in their cellophane bags it was often difficult to hear the stage performers. Afterwards, it was a trip to the fish and chip shop on our walk home.

The few leaves I spent in Bolton, which was also my mother's hometown, gave me a greater appreciation of where my roots were buried and did much to put my personal war into perspective. They brought me back to base a much calmer man.

The only hard part of going to visit Martha was the welcome you always received. Arriving unannounced produced a great loud cry in that peculiar Lancashire accent. "Eeee, it's Doooglass from Canada!" I was then paraded down the street to meet her friends and neighbours. Each would smile, nod, and stare silently at me. Turning to Martha for inspiration on what to say, I would find her also smiling and staring. If a visitor from Mars ever lands in Bolton, I know how he's going to feel.

Leave periods seemed to provide more information about what was going on in the world than we could get in any other way. We read the London papers, listened to the BBC, attended the newsreel theatres, and talked to countless people who were doing all sorts of jobs in military and government positions. It was then you realized how isolated a bomber base could be; how cut off you were from the real world.

There was no appreciation on our base of the war in the Pacific, Burma, and the Middle East, or the war in Russia. The Battle of the Atlantic, which was at its pitch in 1943, got some attention, but it was ill reported and remote. It was only when watching the newsreels that you suddenly understood the horrors of the U-boats or the fantastic flying the Americans were doing off aircraft carriers in the south Pacific.

The London papers had access to the best correspondents ever assembled to cover a war. Bylines by Hemingway, Steinbeck, Ernie Pyle, and Ross Munro, among dozens of others, were daily events. They gave first hand accounts of world actions and they made me realize that Bomber Command wasn't the beginning and end of the war. It was my first introduction to many of those writers and I revelled in their accounts of the war action. But often they wrote side pieces that were just as interesting, and Steinbeck seemed to excel in that regard. One piece he wrote on just general living in England in wartime, stayed in my mind. Describing an Englishman he wrote, "His teeth stuck out so far he looked like a donkey eating bumble bees through a picket fence."

While we waited for our next leave period to roll around, and on those few days we could escape the base between raids, we explored the surrounding villages. Our favourite pub lay in a typical Yorkshire village called Linton-On-Ouse. An old couple ran a rowboat ferry across the Ouse River from a spot behind our barracks. They lived in a small cottage on the far riverbank. After hooting and yelling in the dark, old Ben would emerge and row across to us. Often he had to make several trips to get our gang to the other side. The fare was sixpence but he collected far more than that from appreciative crews. Then we walked to the village and the Alice Hawthorne, where the owner, Ted, and his charming wife, made everyone welcome. It was obvious they liked Canadians and a great rapport developed between us. Tiny Linton had the traditional Maypole set in a central green sward, and shops to service the nearby farming community.

The pub regulars were all farmers. Men, no women. Rough hewn, with hands like leather and red, weather beaten faces, they understood the military. Many had served in World War One and some had medals to prove it. Silver was one of those. He would bring photos of himself to the pub, which showed him dressed in a sergeant's army uniform, wearing the Military Medal. Silver loved the banter of the crews and delighted in our dart tournaments, which he usually won.

One night shortly before Christmas, he asked Bob Oschner, who came from Wetaskawin, Alberta, and me, if we would come to his home for Christmas dinner. We accepted on the spot, even before he told us he was going to serve his biggest goose. Our lips began to smack before he finished the invitation. We showed up at the pub as arranged and after a few, Silver led us across the green to a stone farmhouse, where he introduced us to his wife and son. I still remember that meal.

Wanting to make conversation, I praised the dressing used to stuff the magnificent bird gracing the table. Silver immediately got the idea I loved dressing, preferring it over the goose. He had it backwards, but for the rest of the meal I got nothing but mounds of dressing heaped on my plate. Time after time.

"This one loves dressing, Mother," he said, plunking another yard of dressing on my plate. "Come on then lad, I knows you likes dressing."

Oschner, meanwhile, was gorging on the goose.

Warm hearted, simple, direct, honest people, they had opened their home to us and kept us from getting homesick. There were others just as wonderful. Old Norman, as he was called, was typical. He must have been in his eighties, slow and stiff-walking, but he never missed a night at the Alice Hawthorne. Norman would often slip a small paper parcel into your hand when you were leaving the pub to go home. In it he had wrapped three or four eggs, fresh from his farm. God, how great they tasted when you found a way to cook them.

Our yearning for food had found its way home in letters, and everyone received food parcels from Canada. Some of the contents were strange. An air gunner opened a parcel to find a pumpkin, an unheard of vegetable in Britain. It wasn't large but we reckoned it was sufficient for two pies. Our lips smacked as we took turns holding it and visualizing hot pumpkin pie. But how to cook it?

After a lengthy search an English cook was found who said he knew how to bake pumpkin pies. "Nothing to it, I've made hundreds," he said. Which should have told us something. Negotiations were eagerly entered into and for a certain price he promised to produce the goods. We arranged to do the eating in the back of the mess kitchen late at night.

Three days went by before he passed the word. Tonight. We all gathered in the kitchen where our hero was proudly laying two good sized pies on the table. They smelled delicious and we scrambled for chairs. Pulling up to the table we got our first good look at the pies. Strange, there was a crust over the top of each of them. Oh, well, probably the way they cook them in England, and each of us helped ourselves to a huge slice. I have rarely tasted anything so rotten. We hardly got our forks into our mouths before we were spitting out the pie and yelling at the cook. "What in hell have you done? This isn't pumpkin pie!"

The cook seemed surprised. "I used the pumpkin you gave me."

"But you didn't cook the pumpkin," someone raved at him. "This bloody thing is raw! How did you make it?"

"Just like you make an apple pie. I sliced it up the same way I do the apples. What's wrong?" he demanded.

We had little recourse. The scheme had depended on air force flour and sugar, items strictly rationed, and pilfering was considered a major crime. While we didn't get anything, the English cook got some new words and Canadian expressions he probably still remembers.

Despite the pumpkin pie catastrophe we never gave up trying. Often we would raid a chicken farm late at night and make off with a bird, but the end result, after trying to cook it over an open fire, was always a half-raw, feathered chunk of something inedible.

The 408 squadron badge is a painting of a goose and underneath are the words, "For Freedom." Like so many squadrons, our squadron was adopted by a Canadian town. The good burghers of the adopting towns then took it upon themselves to supply "their" squadron with little extras. Our adopting town had a most direct tie, since we were adopted by Kingsville, Ontario, home of Jack Miner, famed Canadian naturalist, and the man who initiated the banding of wild geese.

When news of this adoption arrived at the squadron there was joy and jubilation as we pictured Christmas and a truckload of geese arriving for the festivities. Our enthusiasm dampened when it was pointed out that Kingsville was a gamebird sanctuary, and a goose a very sacred subject.

We still felt gypped, especially when 419 "Moose" squadron received a ton of moose meat from their adopting city; and 427 "Lion" squadron, that had been adopted by MGM film studios, had a visit from a caravan of movie stars.

Riggers Rare

The winter of 1943-44 produced the worst flying weather England had recorded in a century. Day after day, squadrons were briefed and then stood by to take off at night. Aircraft were bombed-up, standing forlorn in the cold fog and rain of Yorkshire on the hard-stands scattered around the perimeter of the bases. The windsocks stretched taut on their poles, as the dark, rain-swollen clouds half hid them from view. The aircrew were sullen, nervous, and pissed off from attending the lectures laid on when flying was scrubbed. Only the groundcrew continued to work in the mud and cold. Changing bomb loads and gas loads as targets were switched, fighting stubborn engines and instruments that refused to co-operate in the constant dampness. The longer the bombers sat on the ground, the more faults occurred, especially in the electrical circuits; and the groundcrew cursed the weather even more than the target planners in High Wycombe.

Each day Bomber Harris' staff signalled new orders: the target, alternate target, route to be flown, the number of bombers required, types of bomb loads, and actual takeoff and bombing times. Each squadron was required to give a readiness report each day so the planners could determine the force available.

When the trip was scrubbed a different target was selected for the next day. This often meant bomb loads or gas loads had to be changed and the immense task of reloading 800 heavy bombers was borne by the groundcrew. They were nothing short of magnificent.

You had to understand groundcrew, as so many senior officers failed to do. They would literally do anything for you, accept any task, if they knew and understood why it was important, and if they knew you understood their problems. Each of the squadron's twenty bombers was serviced by its own groundcrew. Each crew was headed by a sergeant, although often a corporal was given the responsibility. A flight sergeant or "chiefy" was in charge of each flight of ten bombers. Each small group of fitters and riggers, supported by instrument bashers, radio techs, armourers, and gas crews, owned the bomber. While the aircrew might think the bomber belonged to them, and painted witty sayings, pictures, and bombs on the nose of the bomber, the groundcrew knew differently. It was their aircraft and they had a fierce pride of ownership. They wanted their bomber to work to perfection, and this was apparent to any interested aircrew.

It was easier for non-commissioned aircrew to know and understand groundcrew. For one thing, there was little difference in rank. Communication was therefore easier and much franker. Social evenings together were more frequent, which led to greater understanding and often life-long friendships. If, as aircrew, you understood that the bomber belonged to them, that you only borrowed it for flying purposes, the trust between the ground and air sides developed beautifully.

Often, and against orders, I would let the groundcrew taxi the bomber around the airfield. Air force orders state that only a pilot can move an aircraft under its own power. Groundcrew can start the engines and run them to full power, and they can tow the aircraft around the field; but never are they to taxi the machine so much as an inch. (The same rule applies today and is a colossal waste of time. Pilots being pilots, they are never around when needed.)

Joe Sponarski, of Rainy River, Ontario, was one groundcrew member who delighted in being able to taxi the bomber. Joe was the goalkeeper on the Linton hockey team. We called him the human sieve. There was hardly time for aircrew to play organized sports, but the groundcrews played soccer, baseball, and hockey against other Canadian units. Hockey was the favourite. Many National Hockey players had joined the RCAF and they made the hockey exciting. Milt Schmidt, Porky Dumart, and Bobby Bauer were three pro's who played in Yorkshire. Dumart was based at Linton, while Schmidt and Bauer were at Middleton St. George. All were recreational specialists. Most of the games were played in the rink at Durham. It had been bombed and the roof damaged.

Three huge posts had been positioned down the centre of the ice and four others, two at each end, stood where the defence should have played. They held up the roof but also added an extra dimension to each game of hockey. To watch Milt Schmidt, one of the best centremen ever to play in the NHL, come weaving around those posts at full speed was an awesome sight. At the best of times he was difficult to check, but the seven posts made him unstoppable. There were hilarious moments as checkers ran into the posts while Milt dodged and swerved. Since the posts were frozen, the puck ricochetted off them at great speed and in any direction, sometimes into the wrong net. It was the most entertaining hockey I ever watched and it gave the groundcrew a chance to work off their frustrations.

It was the groundcrew who wept for the missing aircrew as they waited through the long, cold nights for their bomber to return. Aircrew were too busy worrying about their own skins to think overly long about another crew. Not that you didn't miss them, or that their deaths were not felt. You couldn't help noticing the empty beds when twenty-eight or thirty-five guys you lived with weren't there in the morning. But you had your own fears and you knew that tomorrow night you might be listed as "missing in action" or "presumed killed." For the groundcrew it was a sad time when most of the bombers had returned and their dispersal stood empty. Now they had to break in a new aircraft, fresh from the factory, and a new crew, fresh from the Operational Training Unit. Some groundcrew lost ten or more bombers and each had its effect on their behaviour. A pilot gets to love a particular aircraft, for, like a car, it has its own idiosyncrasies; but a ground technician gets to revere it and to give it human qualities.

Each groundcrew was in competition with the other nineteen groundcrews. It became a contest to see which crew could have the bomber that made the most raids. Unstated was the fact that the aircraft had to be successful and return from each raid. So they fussed over their bomber. How they kept them clean in the mud of Yorkshire was a constant mystery. Woe unto the careless aircrew who left even a cigarette butt in their machine.

They worked in rubber boots, turtleneck sweaters, and sleeveless leather jerkins. They would get cold and wet, clambering up the metal scaffolding, changing props or guns or aerials. The two hangars on the base were only used for major overhauls, all other work was done in the open, day or night, rain or shine. Ground-crew were masters of improvisation, designing and making special tools that could make the work go faster. Perhaps the most surprising thing about them was their cheerfulness.

Bomber Harris knew the backbone of his command were these unsung heroes, who worked for years under appalling conditions; and yet, when the campaign medals were handed out at the end of the war, they went unrewarded. Harris was never able to convince Churchill that Bomber Command should be recognized with a campaign ribbon as all other elements of the services were recognized. Perhaps because they never left England they weren't appreciated as fighting troops. But this shameful neglect, so unlike Churchill, is still felt by the survivors of that gallant body of dedicated groundcrew.

Their quarters and living conditions were worse than those of the aircrew; a fact that kept my resentment of the inequality between aircrew officers and aircrew sergeants in better check. Groundcrew could make a pilot aware that he was being too fussy or too concerned in other ways as well. At least my groundcrew had that effect on me. "Tubby" Davidson from Ottawa, a corporal of long standing, had my number.

The Lancaster had a pilot's seat that could be raised or lowered by means of a long handle, much like the parking brake on old cars. Pulling up the lever would ratchet the seat to a higher position. Unfortunately, the ratchet had a habit of slipping.

Taking off in total darkness one night, I reached the end of the runway and pulled the control column back to lift off when my seat crashed to the floor. This put me below the windscreen and the swiftness of disappearing scared the hell out of me. I managed to fly with my hands over my head as we thundered into the blackness, while scrambling to find the lever and jack the seat back into position.

When I mentioned this to Tubby I got his usual reply. "You worry too much." I got the same reply each time it happened and it happened on three occasions. A more forceful request containing an implied threat finally got the problem solved.

I complained to Tubby on another day that the artificial horizon was sluggish and I wanted it changed. "Sure," he replied, "I'll change it in time for tonight's op."

It was a daylight takeoff so climbing out from base and setting course was all done visually. But as we crossed the coast the light faded and I finally turned my eyes into the cockpit to fly on instruments. We never used instrument lights or cockpit lighting of any kind, relying solely on the fluorescence of the instruments. There, staring at me, was a round, black hole in the centre of the instrument panel where the artificial horizon should have been. I jumped a foot. "That bastard Davidson has forgotten to put one in!" I felt with my hand. It was there. Then I realized the dial didn't have fluorescent paint.

When I returned the next morning, I yelled at Tubby about being so bloody stupid. He didn't turn a hair. "You got back, didn't you? You know," he said, "you worry too much."

I didn't get my revenge until several trips later. I had forgotten to take along the pee can and had sat for seven long hours holding a bursting bladder. After shutting down in dispersal, I got out of my seat harness and parachute straps and, kneeling on the seat, fumbled furiously with my fly while sliding open the side window. Finally, I directed a stream towards the tarmac below. Tubby was just coming out from under the bomb bay to tell me there were no bombs hung up.

Ah, sweet relief. Sweet revenge.

You Are Not Alone

The RCAF squadrons in No. 6 Group were situated close to each other; perhaps eight or ten miles separated each base. In some cases the aerodrome landing circuits nearly overlapped. Many pilots, confused by bad weather, thought they were landing at their own base while in fact they were landing at another. Since they were talking to their own control tower, it made for some confusing and dangerous situations. But every landing after a raid was so hectic that errors were ignored. Everyone was relieved if the crews had landed safely somewhere.

With the squadrons so closely packed into that corner of Yorkshire, the impression might be that we all liaised with one another and visited back and forth. Nothing was further from the truth. Each squadron worked in isolation from the others as far as the aircrews were concerned. Engineering officers might confer over mechanical problems; and Group Headquarters were, of course, in contact with each base. But individual crews were very seldom, if ever, in touch.

Our world was Linton and its horizons were strictly limited. Since No. 6 Group was only one of the groups in Bomber Command, the operational briefings referred, if they referred at all, to a "maximum effort" by Bomber Command. Never a reference to what our group was doing, or how many Canadian squadrons or bombers were participating in the raid. It seemed impossible to find out where your old friends were or what they were doing. You would hear that Joe or Sam or some other friend from training days had joined 428 or 419 squadron but rarely did you get a chance to meet. When you did, it was more by chance and often under the strangest circumstances.

One of the brighter Canadians, a kid from Montreal who had left McGill University to enlist, had trained with me. We all considered him special, as indeed he was. In 1939 less than 1 per cent of Canadians had graduated from a university. Hingston wasn't what one would call an athletic type. He looked exactly what he was; a brain. His lack of robust stature led many to mistakenly think he was effeminate. While he looked out of place in the company of his sergeant peers, he revelled in the banter and often the crudeness that surrounded him. We all turned to Hingston in those training days for advice on things above and beyond us. "Hey, Hingston," a voice would yell across the flight room, "how do you spell Madame Tussaud's?"

"What?"

"You know, the wax museum in London."

Hingston would rattle off the spelling and his questioner would unhesitatingly copy it into the letter he was writing home. While he breezed through written exams, Hingston sometimes had difficulty with flight tests and I often wondered how in hell he had got his pilot's Wings. Flying with him was interesting, if sometimes alarming. He had an absolute faith in himself and a total disregard for danger in any form. An aircraft to Hingston was just a machine, like a car. Nothing to get excited about. It wasn't a blind faith but more of a pure belief that flying was quite simple and that he was a natural pilot. One really should spend one's time reading and debating and the flying would look after itself.

I lost touch with him when our training group was split up and sent to various Operational Units. After several months on the squadron I was occupied with more pressing things and Hingston went out of my mind. He reappeared in dramatic fashion one very foggy and rainy day at Linton.

Our flight was sitting around the crew room cursing the weather and pleading with the flight commander to let us take off for local practice. We finally badgered him into calling Flying Control to ask for flight clearance. No dice. The ceiling was estimated at 100 feet in light rain and fog, and control estimated the visibility at 300 yards. Definitely no flying this afternoon, chaps.

As we sat around wondering if the weather would clear in time for an hour's practice, the unmistakable sound of a four-engined aircraft filled the room. It started another round of bitching at the flight commander. "Christ, we must be the only station not flying. How come the other squadrons are up and we're grounded?" Then the aircraft came roaring over our hangar and we all scrambled for the door to see what was going on. We couldn't see any aircraft and the engine noise had died away. We stood in a group on the edge of the grass looking in all directions. The low hanging clouds swirled over the field. Suddenly the noise started again, grew louder, and then passed directly overhead, but no one could see the aircraft. We could tell the noise came from four Merlin engines. No mistaking the growl of a Merlin. We stood there in the rain searching the sky when a Halifax bomber burst into view directly over the runway. "It's a Hally Bag!" someone in the group shouted, as the bomber disappeared into the clouds.

"God, I guess the ceiling *is* low," the flight commander said. "He's only about seventy-five feet and still in cloud." Now station personnel were gathering around our group and the CO and his adjutant arrived in a staff car.

Zoom, the Halifax burst into view. This time between the hangar and the runway, obviously trying to line up with the runway for a landing. There wasn't time to pick out the squadron markings as the plane swiftly disappeared. "He's having a tough time finding the end of the runway," someone exclaimed. The pilots in our group began giving expert opinions of just what the poor pilot should do. "There he comes, he's got the runway now," someone yelled, pointing to our right. The Halifax had set up a really tight circuit and was still turning hard, its port wing down as it crossed the end of the runway. Faintly we could see the black fuselage trying to flatten out for a landing but the runway was still twenty-five feet below.

"You're too hot. Go round again," a voice gave directions. But it was obvious the pilot meant to land on this attempt. We could hear the pop of the Merlins as they were throttled back. Down the runway floated the plane, and then suddenly it dived at the ground, as though the pilot were forcing it down for a landing. *Crunch*, the huge oleo legs of the Halifax rebounded the bomber back into the air. *Crunch* again, as the pilot slammed the aircraft down. We could hear rumblings rolling across the field, sounding like the rattling of a huge tin can. Up the bomber rose, its speed too great for a landing. Now it was eating up space, and either the pilot had to overshoot and try again or the plane would run off the end of the runway. *Bang*, the pilot slammed it hard onto the concrete and we heard the squeal of tires as he immediately applied his brakes.

The Halifax slewed off the runway and started across the grass, directly at our group. *Smash*, the left landing gear snapped and the port wing of the aircraft slid into the ground, the propellers tearing into the grass and the wing tip ploughing a furrow. We ran, scrambling in all directions as the huge bomber slid towards us. Two propellers had taken on pretzel shapes and most of the port wing was twisted back when the shower of dirt, grass, and smoke finally ground to a stop. The port wheel was bounding away across the airfield.

We all stood numbly, silently, staring at our visitor. A popping sound came from the aluminum engine cowlings as they began cooling. No one ran forward and the fire truck had yet to arrive. Then the rear door of the Halifax opened and out stepped the pilot. Seeing our group he headed the few yards towards us. He spotted me about the same time I recognized that walk of his. It was Hingston, smiling and calling out, "Hey, Harve, how are you! God, it's good to see you." I was speechless as we shook hands.

"They tell me you're really getting the ops in," he said. "I've got seven trips done so far. Any of the old gang with you?" He began to reminisce about our training days, completely oblivious of the CO standing next to him trying to get his attention.

"What happened?" I finally managed to ask.

"You mean the aircraft?"

Confused, I nodded.

"Oh, the bloody undercart collapsed on the port side. It snapped off. I thought they were stronger than that. Say, did you hear what happened to Bob Dixon?"

Before I could reply the exasperated CO grabbed Hingston by the arm. "Come over to my office, sergeant, you'll have to fill out a report on this accident." He motioned Hingston towards the staff car.

"Okay," said Hingston, completely unruffled, "I'll come right along." He turned back to me to continue our conversation. This was too much for the CO and he barked at Hingston to move.

"See you, Harve. Say hello to any of the old gang, if you see them." He gave a wave as he climbed into the car.

I never saw him after that, and I learned some months later that he had been shot down over the Ruhr Valley.

Each squadron was almost totally self-sufficient for flying and maintenance purposes. Each had its complement of 500 men and women; and each received its instructions and regulations from No. 6 Group, and its crews and new aircraft from Bomber Command. The tremendous organization that provided everything from paper to planes was hidden from us.

The BBC radio broadcasts would tell us that 800 RAF bombers raided a certain German city, but to those who flew on that particular raid, the announcement seemed academic and statistical, for they might not have seen another aircraft during the seven or eight hour flight. It was rare to see the total force in action, but when you did you witnessed an expression of power so awesome that it never left you. It took a summer evening in double daylight saving time to make it possible.

On short summer nights, Bomber Harris had difficult time limits to meet if the force was to complete a 2,200 mile round trip under cover of darkness. To overcome this handicap he would marshal his force in the air over England in daylight, each bomber setting course at predetermined times as had been programmed at the briefings. Harris wanted a compact bomber stream that would overwhelm the coastal defences and complete the bomb run over the target in twenty-five to thirty minutes. From ten bombers dropping their loads per minute, he gradually increased to thirty bombers per minute, saturating the defences and giving less time for attacks from enemy fighters. To do this, we circled over base, climbing to maximum altitude, until the appointed time came to set course.

Taking off through the rain and gloom of a late Yorkshire afternoon was always depressing. We climbed slowly and laboriously up through 15,000 feet of cloud, the heavily loaded Lancaster straining with its maximum load, inching its way through rain or ice towards the sun above. Sometimes it took an hour to climb 20,000 feet. Slowly, the dark clouds lightened and turned grey, then white, and you knew you were near the tops. Then *pop*, you emerged into the glaring sunshine, so brilliant after the dark of the clouds. As your eyes adjusted to the light, you were able to take them off the instruments and look outside. There you saw a sight that staggered your imagination.

Stretching from horizon to horizon were bombers, hundreds of Canadian bombers, popping up through the clouds, their black bellies stark against the white backdrop of the dazzling cloud tops. Straining up, reaching for altitude, they were all around you. They emerged as if from a magician's hat. Big. Powerful. Sinister. You sat there watching this silent force, milling and circling and finally positioning itself into a stream. Every bomber turning east, all heading exactly where you were headed, towards the German guns. Over 250 strong they finally and convincingly brought home to you the meaning of the bomber stream. You felt a sense of belonging, of being part of a great powerful force, something far more significant than a single squadron.

Steadily, inexorably, they came up out of the clouds. They were in front of you, behind you, on either side, above and below you, stretching out into a stream that would be 100 miles long and five miles wide as it thundered over Germany.

As you flew over the coast of England, you could see to the south 600 RAF bombers streaming northeast to intercept your track, and the stream became a flood and then a torrent as the black bellies turned to join you. Power, tremendous power, deadly power, thrilling in its sense of purpose and might. Radiating strength and togetherness, the message was "you are not alone."

As the sun sank into the clouds behind and the light faded, the bombers in the lead gradually disappeared from sight. Then the ones beside you slowly faded and as the sun set, the ones behind were lost from view and you flew on alone into darkness. Finally, as your aircraft's wings disappeared into the night you were alone with only the roar of your engines and your flickering instruments. Soon you had forgotten the bomber stream as you stared into the blackness, waiting for that first flash of fire from the enemy coast, your mouth drying as you remembered the last time.

Frequently, without warning, the controls were wrenched from your hands, and the Lancaster was thrown up on one wing and heaved over in a terrifying lurch, its overload pushing it out of control. As your heart pounded, and you strained to lift the wing and regain control over this mysterious force, you would suddenly remember the bomber stream. You had hit the slipstream of a bomber directly ahead, the swirling cyclones from its four propellers destroying the smooth air flow over your wings and causing the Lancaster to dive sideways.

No matter how many times it happened, it was terrifying. The swiftness of being pitched up on one wing and the total lack of control in spite of how you tried to correct for it, immediately destroyed your confidence of being in absolute command. It hardly lasted a minute but it seemed to last forever. Afterwards, the consolation was reassuring. You were on track, you were not alone, you had hit the bomber stream, everything was okay. But later you wondered. If you couldn't see a Lancaster, that you knew was there, that had a wing span of 102 feet, how were you going to see a German fighter? Its wing span was only thirty-two feet.

It was rare for our bombers to shoot down enemy fighters, although some gunners shot down two or three, and the incredible Sergeant Peter Engbrecht shot down five and damaged four others. This Canadian gunner received the Conspicuous Gallantry Medal for his unmatched feat but otherwise went unrecognized. He survived the war and remained in the peacetime RCAF as a corporal. Had he been an officer, of course, he would have been widely acclaimed. Most of our fighter pilots never came close to his score of enemy kills.

The average bomber crew never fired at an enemy aircraft, or if they did, failed to hit it. Our 3.03 machine guns were no match for the cannons of the German fighters and everyone knew it. I had some direct experience, myself.

We had just finished a bomb run over Berlin and were heading south away from the raging inferno, when Stan in the rear turret yelled:

"Fighter, six o'clock low, skipper!"

"How far?"

"About 400 yards. He hasn't seen us yet. It's an ME 110. Turn starboard."

I began a turn to starboard, as Stan directed me to the darkest part of the sky. Meanwhile, I strained against my seat straps to turn and look back. I could see nothing. The fighter was beneath us.

"He's staying with us and closing in," Stan warned. Then "Corkscrew starboard, skipper, go!" he yelled; and I could hear his four machine guns roar as he let loose a volley.

"Pull up, skipper," Ken shouted from his mid-upper turret. "I can't get my guns to bear."

I yanked back on the stick and stood the Lanc on its tail, but the fighter was too low and Ken couldn't depress his guns low enough for a shot. Another burst from Stan's guns. "He's hit, skipper, his cockpit lights came on!" I continued to fling the Lanc in a corkscrew all over the sky. Then there was a long continuous burst from the rear turret, the stench of cordite reaching into the cockpit as Stan hosed everything he had at the fighter. "I knocked a rocket off his wing," he called.

"He's burning! He's going down!" Ken screamed, as Stan continued to fire. Then the rest of the crew were yelling, "You've got him, Stan, you've got him!"

I yanked the Lanc to the left in time to see a blazing ball just as it plunged into the clouds. Then a bright red glow lit the clouds from beneath as the fighter hit the ground. As I turned back on course the crew was cheering and congratulating Stan, everyone talking at once. "Good show, Stan," I called, "but keep searching, we may have attracted others." I silenced the babbling, saying, "Save it for debriefing. We still have four hours to fly to get home."

It was evident the fighter had been trying to slip under us for the usual type of attack. Luckily for us it had been outlined by the huge fires of the target. Rarely were they more than quick and silent shadows, flicking down and under as they tried for the unguarded belly of the bomber. Although on occasion you got more than a glimpse.

The roof of the Lancaster's cockpit was covered in perspex so it was possible to see everything above and also to look back down the length of the aircraft. I had hardly settled into the bomb run over Berlin one night, bomb doors open, speed 160 miles per hour, height 20,000 feet, concentrating on the bomb aimer's directions, when something made me look up. A Junkers 88 was crossing directly over my cockpit, going from left to right. The huge Iron Cross on its side looked larger than a billboard. I literally could have reached out and touched it. Three feet lower and it would have smashed directly into us. It was obvious it hadn't seen us and it disappeared into the blackness as suddenly as it appeared.

Another night, this time heading home from Leipzig, we were nicely settled on the home course in total darkness when I noticed a pinprick of light about the two o'clock position. Fascinated, I strained to find out what it was, but said nothing to the crew. Slowly, very slowly, it drew nearer. It appeared to be drifting. A tiny pinprick of light surrounded by blackness. I thought at times I was imagining it. Finally, I could see it was getting closer. It was drifting almost on our exact course, but angled slightly across our track. My God, that's a German fighter's instrument panel! I called the crew's attention to it and they too picked it out.

Ever so slowly, it drifted nearer, until we could make out a full cockpit and the outline of the pilot. It was about twenty-five yards ahead and slightly below, positioned so that we were looking down over the pilot's shoulder. It was a Focke-Wulf 190 travelling at our exact speed.

"Should I shoot it down, skipper?" Steve called from the front turret. Knowing he couldn't hit a bull in the ass with a shovel, I said no.

"Leave it alone, Steve," I ordered. "You'll only miss him and then he'll whip around and nail us."

I turned and flew above and behind the fighter and away from his course. Let sleeping dogs lie, I consoled myself; but I was haunted for the rest of the trip by the thought that maybe we should have fired.

Gunners were a different breed from other aircrew; but rear gunners were different again, even from the mid-upper gunner in the same crew. His position in the rear turret isolated him from the fuselage of the aircraft, while the mid-upper gunner at least had his legs inside the plane. The rear turret extended back beyond the fuselage, and in bombers like the older Wellington with its single tail, the rear gunner couldn't see any part of his own aircraft, no matter how far he rotated his turret.

So tail-end Charlie, as he was called, was left dangling in the dark, pulled along by an unseen force, seeing the war in reverse. His turret was the coldest spot in the unpressurized bomber, and the loneliest. His only connection with the crew lay through the radio intercom. Rear gunners were universally small guys so they could fit into the cramped quarters behind the four machine guns. Here they crouched, stiff with cold, for seven or eight or even nine hours, constantly searching the dark sky. Looking for that quick shadow that could spell death for the bomber.

Rear gunners had their own fraternity, and, like pilots and navigators, had their own jargon. A good one was well respected by his crew, who understood the difficulties he endured. Rear gunners were proud of their position and continually worked to improve their performance. When a gunner discovered his perspex window was always scratched from too much polishing, and, in addition, tended to frost up, he removed the perspex and flew without it. The other gunners followed suit and they all flew exposed to the cold air. While it made them much colder, they felt it gave them a better view. Often they froze their noses or cheeks and sometimes their hands and feet. If they wore electrically heated flying clothes they were free to move properly; but if the power failed, and it often did, they froze. If they wore heavier flying clothes they couldn't manoeuvre freely. If they used too much anti-icing grease on the guns, they would jam. If they didn't put enough on, the guns froze. Too-heavy gloves prevented them from freeing a jammed gun. Too-light gloves and they froze their fingers.

Perhaps their greatest discomfort was the loneliness of sitting in the dark, cut off from sight of fellow crew members, hearing only spasmodic exchanges between pilot and navigator, hour after long, dark hour. But the rear turret was our only effective defensive weapon. The Germans attacked from the rear and from below. With their cannons matched against our machine guns, an exchange of fire was one-sided in their favour.

Stan Campbell, my rear gunner, was a nineteen-year-old kid from Drumheller, Alberta. Tow-haired, freckle-faced, not quite five feet, six inches tall, he typified the rear gunner. His grin extended from ear to ear and he was full of fun and high spirits. Like our mid-upper gunner he had spent only six months in the RCAF before reaching the squadron.

Stan had a very serious side, and he spent much of his free time studying correspondence courses. His father owned a construction business in Drumheller, and Stan wanted to work with his father when he got home. He took courses on every facet of the construction business and drove us all crazy with his exams and tests. How to calculate the amount of concrete needed to make a wall such and such a size. The correct mix of sand and gravel to meet sidewalk specifications. The various stresses in different concrete mixes; it went on and on. Our job, I used to tell him, was to knock buildings down and not to worry about putting them up. He took all the kidding in great style. When he wasn't studying he was writing letters to his family or to his girlfriend, or talking about them.

In the air, Stan was very professional. He never spoke unless it was necessary. Like most gunners he was deluded into thinking he had a competent pilot, and as far as he was concerned, I could fly as low as I wished over the hills or the sea. He revelled in low flying. On takeoff he was in his turret, while a lot of gunners waited inside the fuselage until the bomber was safely airborne before going back to their position.

Stan won the Distinguished Flying Cross for his great work in shooting down the ME 110. He had done it entirely by himself, never giving the fighter a chance to fire as he mowed it down with accurate bursts. He saved our lives that night.

He would read his father's letters to me with great glee, and it was obvious father and son had a marvellous rapport. One letter in particular amused him. His father had written to say a friend had told him how to keep his car windshield clear on frosty Alberta mornings. All one had to do was rub an onion on the glass and it wouldn't frost up. Mr. Campbell had done just that. The onion froze on the glass and unable to see, he ran into a truck. I can still hear Stan laughing.

Stan's father died, just at the time our crew finished our tour of ops, and Stan was sent home immediately to take over the family's business. It was a sad time for Stan but also for the rest of the crew who revered him. It dampened our victory party and our enthusiasm on being "screened" from ops.

Stan will always, to me, symbolize the spirit of that departed breed, the rear gunner. Their trademark was a gung-ho attitude. Fearless and often reckless they tackled the dirtiest and most dangerous job in the bomber with magnificent courage and, being kids, with great style. A lot of them could tell tall tales, spiced and embellished to their own taste in those days when the unusual seemed commonplace. Modesty in personal accomplishments was the order of the day, since everyone was doing something heroic and woe unto the guy who forgot. Everyone descended upon the storyteller with the universal put down, "You're shooting a line." Anyone accused of bragging was challenged immediately, but if the guy persisted the yarn was recorded in a "line book." Most squadrons had one. Here, real or imagined "hairy tales" would be set down describing how the storyteller had outwitted the Germans or had flown in some spectacular fashion. One that I liked concerned a rear gunner who obviously thought of little else but completing his thirty sorties:

BRIEFING OFFICER: Ah, yes, rear gunner isn't it?

REAR GUNNER: Yeah.

BRIEFING OFFICER: Well, ah, did you spot any enemy fighters?

REAR GUNNER: Yeah, I saw an ME 110.

BRIEFING OFFICER: (Sitting up straighter and very interested.) An ME 110? At what range did you spot him?

REAR GUNNER: About 300 yards.

BRIEFING OFFICER: Did he close in?

REAR GUNNER: Yeah.

BRIEFING OFFICER: How close did he come?

REAR GUNNER: I'd say about fifty yards.

BRIEFING OFFICER: (Scribbling madly.) Did you open fire?

REAR GUNNER: No.

BRIEFING OFFICER: Did the ME 110 open fire?

REAR GUNNER: No.

BRIEFING OFFICER: For God's sake, why not?

REAR GUNNER: I figured he was trying to get his thirty trips in, the same as I was.

Hot Air

I found the English people a fascinating study. Their mannerisms were so different and they were so polite. They had a tolerance I found deceptive until I understood that their understated, mild retorts were more devastating than anything I could say. They seldom raised their voices to make a point and I learned to listen. They could be, and they were, maddening, in their seeming disregard of the real facts when I was expounding at great length. But they were seldom rude; only terribly difficult for me to fathom. One trait that I encountered in associating with them was their innate modesty. It had to be encountered first hand to be appreciated.

George Neal was a fellow pilot who came from Hamilton, Ontario. George and I had come to England on the same boat and trained at the same RAF training bases. George, like many Canadians, was from British stock and so had, it seemed, 100 relatives in England. Mothers being what they are, we were all instructed to visit Aunt Mildred or Aunt Agnes and to be sure and look up Uncle Charlie. Letters arrived wondering if you had gone to see them and finally you went. More out of a sense of duty than curiosity.

George had brought his violin along to England. How he managed that I don't know but he would practise day after day, until the whole Nissen hut of airmen would rise up and throw him out. George had gone one Sunday to Birmingham to visit some cousins and he came back to camp to tell me it had been a fair time. They wanted him to return and bring some of his Canadian pals and George asked if I would go with him. Stuck for anything better to do, I said I would.

"I'm going to take my violin along," George said.

"For God's sake, why?" I wanted to know.

"Because they asked me to. It'll be good practice. Anyhow they don't know anything about music."

We got to Birmingham in the afternoon to find the family relaxing in their parlour. We received a warm welcome and had to have tea immediately. Several more of George's relatives arrived and we spent the rest of that afternoon politely answering questions about Canada. They never asked about our flying or directed any questions towards the war. George did most of the talking for us; mostly about his family and all the various relatives. After a dinner which saw nine of us at the table, we relaxed again in the parlour. His aunt then asked George if he would play his violin. After much coaxing and a great display of false modesty, George got his violin and tuned up. George thought he played fairly well and so did I. He began with some semi-classical music and gradually moved into more difficult pieces, while the relatives raved and applauded. Lost in this adulation, George seemed willing to play all night. But he finally sat down after an hour, flushed with pleasure at the compliments that poured over him. He was ready at any moment to do it again, if they would only ask.

After a polite interval, a cousin asked if she could try George's violin. George was delighted and gave her some preliminary instructions on how to hold it correctly, which the girl accepted with interest and courtesy. "I think you'll find," said George, "that if you hold your elbow like this," and he demonstrated where her elbow should be, "it will make it easier to hold the violin." His cousin thanked him politely, as George continued to flutter around her, arranging the music on the stand.

"I think I'll try Mozart's Concerto No. 4," the cousin said, tuning the strings. I looked over at George and found he had a tolerant smile on his face. He caught my eye and winked.

I am no music critic but I know excellent music when I hear it. I heard it that evening. She was fantastic. As she played I continued to look towards George. He seemed to grow smaller and smaller, the grin gone from his face and replaced with a puzzled expression.

We all applauded enthusiastically after her number. The cousin, about eighteen years old, blushed and said, "I'm afraid I'm out of practice. Here George, you play again." George declined, saying he would rather hear her play some more. So an uncle took the violin and played several pieces in the same brilliant manner as the cousin. Then his aunt played it and gave an even better performance. Eventually every one of them played at least one piece. But they couldn't coax George to play, as hard as they tried. He sat there trying to make the best of a bad situation.

On the train going home he was a little more voluble. "For Christ's sake, they led me right up the garden path! I didn't know any of them could even whistle. And to think I told her how to hold the goddamned thing. Oh, Jesus," he moaned.

It took time to get used to the English and their ways, so different from what we knew in Canada. It wasn't one-sided, of course. The staid RAF officers, especially the more senior ones, failed completely to understand the young, brash Canadian kids. When the two sides met, it often proved interesting.

In an RAF mess, one of the ploys used to keep those bloody colonials in their place was the ultimate British put down: acting as though you weren't there. Those Canadians foolishly intent on demanding better meals or some amenity thought vital, got that treatment. Upon rising to speak, the Canadian would see newspapers opening in front of the RAF types. When he had finished speaking the RAF types folded their papers. The meeting then resumed from the exact point that had been reached before the Canadian had spoken.

Most of the Canadian bases had RAF administrative officers in key positions. Our base had about 1,500 all ranks, and about 100 were RAF. On the whole they were decent and reasonable but there were notable exceptions. Many of them had years of service and found it impossible to understand how those bloody Canadians had risen to their present ranks at such a young age. And, by God, some of them were senior officers!

We had an RAF Wing Commander on our base who was very starchy. He also had a very short fuse. Anything contrary to regulations lit that fuse. One summer day he was working in his ground floor office, when a Lancaster taxied in to park just outside his open window. The pilot gunned an outer engine to swing the aircraft, and then revved all four engines wide open to move forward and park. A blast of leaves, dirt, and grass showered the building and most of it landed on the Wing Commander's desk.

Overcome with rage, he hurled himself through the window and marched to the rear door of the Lancaster. The door finally opened and the pilot appeared, shoving out the short ladder. The

Wing Commander opened fire immediately and his tirade continued as the pilot descended the ladder.

The Wing Commander wanted to know who could have been so bloody stupid to rev an engine alongside a building? Of all the moronic things he had ever seen, this had to be the dumbest. The pilot really took the bloody cake. His balls were going to serve as bookends. . . . The Wing Commander was just getting nicely into his subject when the pilot reached up, removed helmet and goggles, and shook out the most gorgeous head of blonde curls.

Speechless, his mouth agape, the blushing officer turned and fled.

The pilot was a member of the Air Transport Auxiliary (ATA) who was delivering a factory fresh Lancaster to the squadron. Denied the right to fly in combat the women pilots of Britain and America had formed air transport units. They did a brilliant job of ferrying every type of aircraft, from the fastest Spitfires to the largest bombers. It is amusing to hear in this day and age the old male arguments arise when girls ask to fly in the armed services. Anyone who watched the ATA girls handle wartime aircraft could verify the ease with which they did a very difficult job. Besides, anyone who could make an RAF Wing Commander speechless had to be something special.

Royal Air Force characters weren't confined to officers. The gnarled and seasoned warrant officers, particularly the discips who marched us around, had their own special expressions. Most of them had been in the service twenty years and some had joined as boys at sixteen, under an apprenticeship plan. They had seen and heard it all, and they blistered our ears on every occasion.

One sergeant-major had a vocabulary unique by any standard. He marched a squad of us to church one day to attend a funeral parade. As he led the squad to the church door, he stepped aside, but kept the left, right, left, right cadence going as we proceeded inside. A sergeant in front of me tried to enter wearing his cap but the sergeant-major snatched it off his head roaring, "Take yer fuckin' 'at off in the 'ouse of God, cunt!" Oh, those English. We would learn lots more about them as the war progressed.

There were more English women in the pubs than English men, which, I suppose, was natural with so many of the men serving overseas. But an additional factor was the air raid duties that all civilian men were forced to perform. Mostly these were office workers who spent four or five hours every night on the roof tops or working in and around air raid shelters. Each wore a tin helmet and an armband, and each carried a bucket of sand and a stirrup pump to smother incendiary bombs. It was cold, dreary, and often very dangerous work, standing on the roofs or patrolling the blacked out streets. Sometimes they worked all night, digging for bodies, putting out fires, and helping the wounded to first aid stations. A large number of Canadian fire fighters had volunteered for duty in London and they, too, did yeoman service, also with little recognition for their dangerous and courageous work.

The wives of the volunteers were, to use their expression, browned-off that their husbands had these constant night duties. They would sit in the pubs and growl about the bloody war, the bloody Germans, and bloody Herbert, who was never home.

Some of my visits to London were in the company of another guy called George. He was not at all like George Neal, (as the English would say, he was "a different cup of tea"). He was the best looking RCAF type I ever knew. The girls found him irresistible. He got all the girls and I paid for all the beer, or so it seemed to me. But he was fun to be around. We had barely settled into a pub one night when we were invaded by four air raid widows. They were in good form and had been into the beer long before we arrived. George, as usual, got all the attention and one wife in particular really came on strong. It wasn't long before she invited George home.

"Come on with me, love," she said. "Alf is doing his bloody warden job and won't be home till morning. I like you Canadians," she added. The rest of us at the table laughed as they got up and left, and we soon forgot them.

It must have been an hour later when George arrived back on the dead run. He was in stocking feet, his shirt hanging out from his open tunic. "God," he said, "that was close!"

We all asked questions at the same time. "Give me a beer, first," he said. Wiping the sweat from his face and gulping the beer, he went on, "Her husband caught us."

"But I thought she said her husband was doing warden duty? How did he catch you?" I asked.

"He had forgotten his wrist watch and came home to get it and just walked into the bedroom. God, he sure gave me one hell of a kick in the ass before I could get out. I left my boots under the bed. Jesus, what am I going to do?" We all roared with laughter.

"Go back and get them," I said.

"Oh, sure, just knock on the door and ask for my boots, I suppose."

It seemed everyone in the pub had to hear the story and a crowd gathered around our table, everyone offering advice to the distraught George. After a few more beers, George calmed down and began to think about what to do. He looked funny sitting there without his boots on and I couldn't help thinking that at long last George had got his. One of the RCAF types who had joined our table was a heavy-set sergeant. He couldn't understand why George hadn't socked the husband.

"How big is the guy?" he asked George.

"Christ, I don't know. I was too busy scrambling into my clothes and trying to get out of the house," George said irritably. "You guys think this is funny but you didn't run half a mile in your stocking feet. I damn near broke my neck running in the blackout."

"Let's go back," said the big sergeant, whose name was Art. "I'll knock on the door, and when the husband comes out, I'll pick a fight with him. Then you run in and get your boots. Do you remember where the house is?"

"Yeah, I'm pretty sure I can find it. But do you think it will work? I don't want to tackle the guy. I can still feel that kick in the ass."

"Hell, he can't be that big. I'll just scuffle with him to give you time to dart in and grab the boots." It seemed obvious that Art was looking forward to meeting the husband.

It seemed just as obvious that George was not. "Are you coming with us?" George looked at me.

"Not on your life, mate. I'm quite happy right here."

After going over their plan a few more times and with additional fortification, George and Art put down their glasses and left. The rest of us chattered away imagining the beating that George might get, but in less than half an hour they returned in high spirits. George, wearing his boots and roaring with laughter, was pounding Art on the back and congratulating him on a successful sortie.

"Piece of cake," he yelled. "Art really gave the husband a

going-over and the old girl had my boots ready behind the door. God, she even took a few whacks at him herself. The beer's on me," he chortled.

English pubs. What would we have done without them?

Several of the WAAF's I pubbed with in London worked as crews on barrage balloons. These were the enormous, gas-filled balloons that floated over every major city in England. The Germans also used them in their air defence network. If an aircraft flew low over a city, so the theory went, it would hit the steel cable that anchored the balloon to the ground. Some aircraft did crash when they hit them, but surprisingly, others hit the cables and flew home with great pieces torn off a wing. Our bombers were equipped with cable cutters positioned in slots on the leading edges of the wings. The cable, if it slid along the wing, would fall into one of these slots and be severed by a powerful spring-loaded chisel. To test whether the theory worked, we would climb up on ladders and jam heavy screwdrivers into the slots. They worked like magic, and would cut the strongest screwdrivers.

To help avoid our own balloons each aircraft was fitted with an anti-balloon warning horn. If you inadvertently flew over an English town the screecher would sound. A high, piercing scream filled the cockpit and with your heart in your mouth you turned away. On a clear day they didn't present a problem for you could see them swaying in the wind, looking like great pillows. But most often they were buried in thick cloud, and your imagination heightened the alarm of the screecher.

When the girls asked me one night if I would like to see their balloon unit and watch them launch one, I jumped at the chance. Early next morning they sent a van to collect me, and I was driven to their small unit on the southern outskirts of London.

The unit lay in a strip that extended from London to the south coast. It was called buzz-bomb alley, so named for the route flown by the pilotless V-1 rockets that Germany was launching by the hundreds, all targeted for London. The three girls were busy when I arrived, gassing up their balloon. It had been damaged by lightning and they had winched it down for repairs. Now it was ready to be launched again and I was in time, they said, to help get it airborne. It was a beautiful August day and they were working in shirt sleeves, their ties and jackets discarded. I took off my tunic and, rolling up my sleeves, lent a hand. After the pump was running smoothly there wasn't much we could do but wait. The girls decided a cup of tea would be just the thing so we retired to their small quarters. No luck, they were out of tea. It was then that Alice, who had extended the invitation to me, thought of the gin she was saving for a birthday party. "Would you care for a gin?" she asked. After the night in the pub it was exactly what I wanted. She found the precious bottle she had been hoarding for the party and poured the four of us hefty drinks. We took them outside and sprawled in the grass to enjoy the welcome sunshine.

The girls gave me a rundown on how they operated the balloon, the maintenance schedule, how many there were around London, and how boring it was.

"There's never any excitement to this job," Alice complained.

At that exact moment, a buzz bomb roared into view with a fighter plane in hot pursuit. There was a terrific explosion and the V-1 blew up in a great ball of fire. One for our side, and we all cheered the fighter pilot who had prevented the flying bomb from reaching London. I turned to Alice. "How much excitement do you want? That crazy doodle-bug could just as easily have landed here."

"Oh, you get used to those silly things," Alice replied. "We pay no attention. What I meant is the bloody day after day of the same boring work. When will it ever end? I've been stuck here for two years. Most of the girls I joined up with are on fighter or bomber bases. They have a wizard time, what with dances, parties, and bags of men all around. I'm stuck here looking after a bloody bag of gas." Her two companions nodded in moody agreement.

"By the way," I inquired, "when do we send the balloon up?"

"Oh, it's not nearly ready yet. It takes a long time to fill it. Here, relax and have another gin."

"How about your sergeant. Where is he?"

"Don't worry about him. Alex is off today. Not supposed to be when we're launching, but we've got it taped."

"He hardly ever comes around anymore," added Jean, a tall, thin girl. "We can handle everything, anyhow. Alex only narks about something or other when he's here. We never bother about him."

The third member of the unit, Nancy, chimed in with, "When the winch breaks down or the pump needs servicing we call him, but except for that we don't really need him."

"How high do you fly it?" I wanted to know.

"Anywhere from 2,000 to 5,000 feet, although it varies," Alice replied, "but it can go a lot higher."

"God," I said, "wouldn't it be great to go up on it. Imagine sitting on top, drifting back and forth . . . It would be like sitting on a pillow, floating around with the clouds. Say, has anyone ever gone up on one?"

"We haven't," Jean said, "but I've heard people have ridden them on other units." We were now well into the gin, as we lay basking in the sun.

"Well, I sure would like to have a go," I said.

"Why not," Alice agreed, sitting up suddenly. "I reckon we could winch it up slowly. Maybe only, say, 1,000 feet. Would you really like a ride?"

I hesitated. "Well, sure, but if anyone found out, you'd all catch a packet."

"Oh," Alice said, "who's to know? We can get away with it."

I could feel the gin fading. What if I fell off? It would be the first time I had ever flown without a parachute. The girls were looking at me. I gave a laugh and said, "Sounds like great fun. But how about you coming with me?"

Alice didn't hesitate. "What a marvellous idea! Yes, let's."

"You're kidding?"

"No, I'm not. I've often wondered what it would be like to sit on that bag, away up there, where no one can see me."

"Okay," I said, "you're on. But how do we sit on the damn thing?"

"I think it would be better if we didn't fill it right up. Say about three-quarters full, and then we'll sink in and not roll off. But it has to have a certain amount or it won't fly properly. I don't think you'd better winch us up too high," she informed Jean and Nancy. "We may want to come down in a hurry."

Finishing our drinks, we walked over to the balloon, which was now about two-thirds inflated, looking like a giant sausage as the gas hissed into it. The girls began disconnecting the hose and readying the winch as Alice gave instructions on how fast to raise the balloon.

"Now mind, stop if you hear me yell and no more than 1,000 feet. If you see anyone coming, or if the wind gets up and the weather changes, pull us down straight away!"

Giggling, we arranged a ladder, and holding onto each other for support we climbed on top of the bag. It was difficult walking as we sank into the partially filled balloon. By holding onto each other we managed to work our way slowly to the centre. We sat down when we thought we were in the middle.

"Righto," cried Alice to the two girls, "start us up!"

A groaning noise came from below as the winch began revolving. Very slowly we began to ascend. We could see only the sky above with the summer clouds drifting along. There was no sensation of movement. It felt wonderful. As we rose higher the balloon began to sway gently in the wind. The noise of the winch floated up to us and we could hear the excited voices of Nancy and Jean as they cautioned each other on how fast to release the cable. Alice and I lay back and put our arms around each other. We were both smiling. "Frightened?" I asked.

"No, this is absolutely marvellous."

"I wonder if we're the first to do this?"

"From stories I've heard," said Alice, "I hardly think so. But wouldn't it be an absolute laugh if we were the first."

"No way we'll ever know, but who cares. I could stay here forever. What a way to fly! No bloody parachute or Mae West or seat harness to bind you. No engines roaring. No crew to worry about. We're as free as the birds!" I began rolling around to test what would happen if we moved suddenly. Nothing. The balloon was perfectly stable. I rolled back to Alice and put my arms around her. "Wouldn't this be the perfect place to have a go?"

"You must be a mind reader," Alice replied, returning my kisses and snuggling closer as I began to unbutton her shirt.

We rolled and tossed on top of the balloon for two golden hours, the sun streaming down, the balloon swaying gently, and the clouds drifting by. Heaven. What war? Was there really a war on?

"There's A War On!"

To ask for anything in wartime England was to be greeted with the words, "Don't you know there's a war on?"

More surprisingly, you received that admonition even on your own base. Since we were flying night operations it was essential to have lights in the flight rooms. Nothing fancy, just plain lightbulbs naked and glaring from the ceiling. Our lightbulb burned out one day and Hal Miles, the flight commander, suggested I go to the supply section and get another. It seemed a simple enough request and yet I thought I detected something more when he suggested I be the one to run the errand. "Make sure you take the old one, or they won't give you a new bulb," he said.

I walked around to the main supply building and went in. Clerks were busy logging newly arrived items and putting them on shelves, opening crates, and counting things. I stood there for some time before anyone paid any attention to me. Finally, a corporal came to the counter and asked what I wanted. I held up the old bulb and said I would like a new one.

"A new bulb?" asked the clerk, sounding as if I had asked for his wife. "You want a new bulb?"

"For Christ's sake, corporal, are you deaf? Yes, I want a lightbulb. Here's the old one."

"Well, just a minute," he said. "I'll have to see the Squadron Leader about this." He disappeared down a hall and returned shortly. "Sorry, sergeant, but you can't have a new bulb."

Dumbfounded, I stared at him. "What in hell do you mean, I can't have a new bulb. Are you sick? This bulb is burned out and I want it replaced. Get me a new one. Now!"

"Sorry, sergeant, but the Squadron Leader says no." The corporal turned to leave and I reached over the counter and grabbed his shoulder.

"Get me the Squadron Leader."

In a few minutes the Squadron Leader came to the counter, a scowl on his face. He glared at me and said, "Look here, sergeant, don't you know there's a war on?"

"Sir," I replied, "I think I do. But you had better know that if I don't get a new lightbulb we can't sign out the crews tonight. The CO will want to know why we didn't go on ops."

The Squadron Leader turned away silently, and in a few minutes the corporal came back with a bulb and asked me to sign for it.

When I returned to the flight room, Squadron Leader Miles said in amazement, "You got one! Christ, you're the number one scrounger on the squadron. How did you do it?"

It was my baptism into the stupidities of a flying base where the sharp end of the air force was treated by the support troops as a nuisance.

The cooks in the air force hated aircrews to a man. Why, they complained, can't the aircrew eat at regular meal times?

Why, said the stores officer, can't those bloody aircrew understand I'm closed for five days taking inventory?

Why, said the paymaster, can't they attend my normal pay parades, like everyone else?

Why, said the transport officer, should we pick up aircrew? Why can't they take the scheduled bus?

Why, said the base commander to his squadron commanders, weren't your crews on parade this morning?

Why, said the non-flying officers, can't the aircrew do orderly officer duties, like we do?

Why, said the medical officer, can't they attend at normal sick parade hours?

Why, said the aircrew, can't those stunned bastards understand what our job is?

On a well run base those problems were handled by a CO who understood both sides of the question and made sure everyone else understood. If you were supporting personnel, by God, you supported. If you were aircrew, by God, you flew, day or night, around the clock. Both sides had better understand the sole reason for the base was the bombing of Germany.

It was only one of the many mysteries of wartime England that you encountered in various forms. It sprang from an individual's lack of control over anything. Everyone seemed a tiny part of a great mass with little independence concerning his own actions.

I was standing at a pub bar one night, talking to the owner, who was pulling on the huge handles that dispensed the keg beer. A small man came and stood beside me. He was dressed in a tweed jacket and cloth peaked cap that matched his plus fours. He ordered a pint of mild and bitter in a recognizably Scottish accent. The publican took a glass and slowly pumped out the beer, careful to let the froth subside as he neared the rim. The Scot, whose chin barely came above the bar, was watching. Then he carefully counted out twelve pence and lay the money on the bar. The owner set the glass of beer down with a, "Righto, sir, there you are, then."

The Scot stood silently eyeing the glass of beer. As the foam finally settled, he said, "Do you think you have room to get a wee drop of whiskey in there?"

The publican studied the glass. "Aye, I think I could."

"Well then," said the Scot, "fill it up with beer."

Intrigued, I fell into conversation with the Scot as we drank our beer, inquiring about various areas of Scotland. I had long wanted to visit Glasgow, and if there were characters like this guy, I wanted to meet them.

On my next leave I headed north on the Flying Scot, which ran between Glasgow and London and was the supreme train in all of England. It wasn't much in wartime, but it was fast and that helped. After wandering around Glasgow for a few days I got restless and headed by bus out to see the other cities, crossing over to the east coast and Aberdeen and Edinburgh. There I was in striking distance of the Royal and Ancient Club of St. Andrews, the golfclub mecca of all true golfers. I wanted to play the Old Course, but without clubs thought there was little chance. Nothing ventured, nothing gained, so I boarded a train to try. My first impression was the same one recorded just a few years later by Sam Snead. On catching a glimpse of the famous links from his train window, Sam had said, "That looks like an abandoned golf course."

I got a warm welcome from the club and they soon had me outfitted with clubs and a few scarred and cut golfballs. Since production had been halted for the duration of the war, golfballs were in very short supply and each one was used until its cover disintegrated.

Built on the side of the sea, St. Andrews is a true golf links, its fairways carved out of the old sand dunes. Open to the winds sweeping in from the sea, it challenges you from all directions. The public have the right to use the course as a park, and actually have the right of way. I was playing with three other servicemen who, like me, had long wanted to play this famous course while they had the chance. Often our play was interrupted by mothers pushing baby carriages across the fairways.

As our foursome waited on the tee for a group of young children to move out of range, I was gazing towards the sea and the sand dunes along the shore. There, a long line of donkeys with riders was meandering along. Puzzled, I turned to my caddy, a middle-aged man wearing a vest and suitcoat, a collar and tie, and the universal cloth peaked cap.

"What," I asked, pointing at the donkeys, "are they?"

"Oh, aye," he said, "them's the town council."

Yankees Doodle Dandy

Hundreds of our bombers were lost over England trying to land in fog and foul weather. Our crew seemed to land at a strange base on about half of our trips, diverted from home base by bad conditions. While weather was a major factor in landing elsewhere, it was also often caused by damaged aircraft that refused to fly anymore, or by a shortage of gas.

Whatever the cause, we always tried to land at an American Eighth Air Force base – not only to see the Fortresses and Liberators, but to get some of that American food. Unbelievable corn on the cob, real hotdogs, and, by God, ice cream in all flavours! Iceberg lettuce. Hamburgers. If you had to stay for a day or so there were first run movies, or American actors and performers putting on skits. But the food was the real reason for our visits. What a treat after all our brussels sprouts, mutton, and potatoes; not to mention the custards covering everything called dessert. Landing at a Yank base was like playing hookey from school and brought back all the memories of home, now so far behind us. It was entirely childish and viewed as such by the senior ranks, but to us it was a touch of realism. The RCAF issued orders against landing at any American base. Why they thought we would be contaminated was difficult to fathom. We thought our leaders too stupid to ship over Canadian food or liquor, even though our commanders railed at the British for not giving Canada more control of her forces. Had Mackenzie King brought over some booze and handed it around, or made any effort to send Canadian food, the troops wouldn't have booed him so much.

The Yanks were overly generous with everything they had, from food to their excellent flying suits. They would hand over a beautiful, leather, sheepskin-lined flying jacket without hesitation. They loved to look at the Lancaster, especially the thirty-two foot bomb bay, and would crawl all over our kite while we scrambled aboard the Liberators and Fortresses. We marvelled at the heavy machine guns which stuck out from all angles. They bristled with fire power. We were impressed. No wonder they shot down so many German fighters.

One of the more interesting differences was the flak jacket issued to each American crew member. These were sophisticated bullet proof vests: heavy, sleeveless jackets with hundreds of small armour plates quilted into heavy canvas. When we asked about them the Yanks demonstrated how they were worn. But one enterprising pilot told me, "Hell, I don't wear the damn thing. I fold it up and sit on it. No use leaving your vital parts exposed."

We were even more impressed with the cockpits of their aircraft. The Liberator bomber in particular had the greatest set of pilots' seats of any aircraft. Huge leather creations, they looked like barber chairs. Here was a basic difference in how Americans built aircraft and how the British built them. The Brits built the complete aircraft and then stood back to admire their work. Only then did they exclaim in surprise, "Oh, goodness, I think we have forgotten the cockpit. Perhaps we should cut a hole in the front somewhere and put in a bench for the pilot." The Yanks, on the other hand, built the aircraft around the cockpit.

Another difference was the idea that two pilots were better than one, especially when you were trading bullets with an enemy. Many American pilots were wounded or killed and yet the kite came home, flown safely by the second pilot.

An additional reason for landing at the American bases was to look up old buddies who had trained with the RCAF but had transferred to the Eighth Air Force when it began operations in England. In 1940-41, before America went to war, thousands of American kids had come north to Canada to get their Wings in the RCAF. They added a new dimension to the force, their lifestyles a refreshing change from the more stolid Canadian approach. Almost every RCAF training course had five or six Yanks, not to mention Australians or New Zealanders, and their reactions, first to Canada and the RCAF, and then to the Brits and the RAF, were a constant source of amusement and delight.

As America got deeper into the war and finally formed the

Eighth Air Force in England, the Yanks flying with the RCAF and RAF were offered the opportunity of transferring to the Fortress and Liberator squadrons. This meant immediate promotion to lieutenant for the sergeants and a huge jump in pay. Not to mention the jazzy uniform and food. The lure was generally irresistible, especially the thought of being among their own countrymen.

Surprisingly though, many stayed right where they were, in the RAF or RCAF, strongly attached to their crews and determined to complete a tour of ops before transferring. They realized they would be promoted, but they also knew they would be second pilots and no longer captains of aircraft. We had several Yanks on our squadron and one even finished a tour. A tall, skinny kid from Oklahoma, Mike Humphreys typified the Yanks we knew. He suffered every conceivable disaster in the air, from ditching in the North Sea to getting shot all to hell on several occasions and wobbling back to base on two engines. Early one morning he staggered in from a raid on Hamburg. He had been hit by lightning and two engines had been knocked out. They were still ice-covered when he landed.

Mike wore his pants about two inches above his shoes. High water pants he called them. He was revered by his crew and except for his western twang when he spoke, seemed indistinguishable from them. Many of the Americans in the RCAF were southern boys, and they suffered from the damp and cold of England even more than we did. The English girls were fascinated by them, even though they had difficulty understanding the slow, drawling speech.

Red Morgan was a Texan who had trained with us in Canada. Six feet four inches and well over 230 pounds, strong as an ox, redheaded and freckled, he had a grin a mile wide and a slow, diffident manner that charmed everyone. Always front and centre at every party, Red could outdrink all of us. And he was stubborn as a mule.

Red was one of the first to transfer to the Eighth Air Force, and it was the thought of bourbon whiskey that decided the issue. "If'n I'm ever gonna get me another drink of bourbon, I'd better join them Yanks," he drawled. He was given the rank of second lieutenant and appointed second pilot in a B-17 Flying Fortress squadron. Red led a charmed life in those vicious daylight raids the Americans fought all over Europe. Bits and pieces of information would filter through to us on their progress, and we often exchanged letters with some of our ex-companions. But their losses were just as high as ours and eventually the mail stopped. Just the same, we all heard about Red.

On a raid deep into Germany, he was flying as co-pilot when the formation was overwhelmed by German fighters. His captain was hit in the head by a cannon shell which by some fluke didn't kill him – but rendered him insane. He continued to fly the bomber with blood all over him, and his wild efforts to keep the Fortress in formation plunged the bomber dangerously close to the other aircraft. He clearly had no conception of what was happening.

Red took control from the co-pilot's seat, or at least he tried, for the captain wouldn't release the controls and was immune to Red's cries to let go. Reaching over, Red pressed the captain back off the control column while he flew the bomber in formation with his right hand. They still had miles to go to the target and were under heavy attacks from the German fighters, something which kept the rest of the crew from lending assistance. Red flew, holding off the struggling captain, bombed the target, and brought the aircraft home to base. It wasn't until several hours after leaving the target that the captain died and the crew had a chance to lift him to the back of the aircraft. Through all this time Red had held the pilot away from the controls and flown the Fortress without colliding with his own bombers.

Red received his country's highest award, the Congressional Medal of Honor, for that day's work, and went on to finish the war in one piece. When the news hit our squadron we were as thrilled and as proud of him as were his own people.

Arnold Rose was another Yank who had joined the RCAF and had graduated as a pilot with me. He was sent overseas along with the rest of us and had great difficulty understanding the English and their ways – especially the English sense of humour. Rose was a very serious minded individual who thought the war a desperate struggle against tyranny and couldn't understand his own country's reluctance to get involved. Like so many of us he saw the war as completely black and white, perceiving the Nazis as a threat to freedom everywhere. This strong belief had brought him to Canada to join forces against Hitler's power, and he relished the idea of being in England where he could fight against it.

We were standing at the bar of a pub one night, enjoying the convivial atmosphere, when we were joined by two English couples. They were married and about ten years older than ourselves. We struck up a friendly conversation and exchanged drinks with them. The two ladies were drinking Pimm's, a popular fruit-based cocktail. Pimm's had four or five different liquor bases and the ladies took it upon themselves to explain the mysteries to us. Rose was intrigued with the explanations and happily joined in the friendly talk, losing his normal reserve towards strangers. The conversation finally got around to the fact that he was an American serving with the RCAF, and this drew interest and exclamations from the Brits. One of the wives asked Rose where he came from in the United States.

"Massachusetts," Rose said.

"What?" they all asked. "Where did you say?"

"Massachusetts," he repeated.

"Massa-two-shits," squealed one of the wives. "Massa-two-shits!" She was screaming with laughter, as the crowd in the pub turned their attention to her. "Massa-two-shits," she bellowed, completely out of control. "Oh, I say, can you imagine? Massa-two-shits!" Everyone nearby joined in laughing at this English voice and her pronunciation of the word.

Rose was furious. "For Christ's sake, what's funny?" he demanded of the laughing women. "Come on," he yelled at me, "we're going. Bloody stupid limeys, they make me sick!" Rose dragged me towards the door. "We should let them fight their own goddamned war. Stupid bastards!" He continued raving until we got to the next pub.

Escape Artists

On "stand down" days, those days when the weather was terrible, even for local flying, the aircrew attended lectures. Perhaps the most interesting were the escape and evasion talks, given by aircrew who had found their way home to England after baling out over the Continent.

We all carried escape kits when flying ops. These contained foreign money (Belgian and French francs, German deutschmarks), and a map of Europe printed on silk. Several buttons on our battledress were actually compasses. When the button was balanced on a pin, it revolved until it pointed to magnetic north. Hard candy and chocolate completed the kit. The goodies were packed in a small canvas pouch which you stuffed into your battledress blouse before takeoff.

The lecturers had all managed to bale out of stricken aircraft and successfully evade capture. Most had found the French Underground agents and had been smuggled through France and into Spain. Some had taken months to reach England, but others took only a few weeks. It depended upon the help they received from sympathizers. The majority of the would-be evaders, of course, were caught by the Germans, and often their benefactors were shot. It was a desperate business as the German SS troops tried to destroy the pipelines to freedom. They dealt with the underground workers in ruthless and unmerciful fashion.

Everyone making it back to England was awarded a badge called the Order of the Flying Boot. This cloth badge, which depicted a winged boot, was proudly displayed on the pocket of their tunics, under their Wings.

It took a very dedicated and brave soul to suffer the destruction of his aircraft, parachute into the night, collect his wits, and then hide from the Germans. Alone, scared, unable to speak any of the languages, unsure of exactly where he was, or in which country for that matter, he had to hide by day and travel by night. Often he had lost his flying boots when he baled out, or was not dressed for living outdoors in winter. Cold and hungry, he would call at the first farmhouse, hoping to get assistance. Often he was aided, but more often he was turned over to the German authorities, the fear of reprisal paramount in the farmer's mind.

Those who returned had marvellous tales to tell, but security forbade the exposure of many valuable parts. They were allowed to tell us how to recover from the initial shock of landing at night by parachute: to bury the parachute in a certain way immediately upon landing; to keep away from roads and instead to use the fields. They told us when to move and when to hide; and about the help we could expect from the underground once in contact. But they were forbidden to talk about people or places where the underground operated.

Some had been stuck in a particular town for months, hiding in cellars or attics. Some had posed as priests, others as deaf-mutes or blind persons. All carried false identification papers prepared for them by the underground. The odd fortunate would tell of being held in a house that contained only women, which captured everyone's attention and took away some of the dread of being a fugitive.

Bits and pieces of these lectures stayed in your mind and made you determined to escape if you got shot down. "Don't ever leave your knife and fork side by side on your plate when eating in a restaurant. The French always place the knife and fork across the centre of the plate, one pointing at the other. The Gestapo will be looking for such clues. Don't trust anyone. Gestapo members will pose as underground workers to trick you. Remember, if captured, give only your rank, name, and serial number." The realities of escaping proved more difficult than I realized when listening to those lectures, but luckily I didn't learn about them until the war was over and some of my friends returned from the POW camps.

Ted Griffen was an American kid who trained with me at several RCAF bases and we ended up at Linton to do our operational flying. Ted was a member of 426 squadron. He was shot down on a raid to Frankfurt just a few days before Christmas in 1943. An excellent pilot, Ted was determined to evade capture and I used to think that if anyone could manage the trick, it would be him.

He told me this story in 1945.

"Two German fighters attacked us just as we swung away from the target. They knocked out three of our engines and started a fire in one of them. I ordered my crew to bale out for we were losing height rapidly. I managed to get the engine fire out with the automatic fire extinguisher as the crew baled out.

"After they had gone I got out of my seat and stood in the aisle, flying the Lanc with one hand while I collected my wits. I knew the Belgian border was only about 100 miles from Frankfurt. If I could get over the border I knew I would have a better chance of escaping. But I didn't know how far I could fly the Lanc on only one engine. I was determined not to be taken prisoner and began checking to see that I had my escape kit and anything else I could cram into my jacket. I managed to reach back and grab the navigator's maps and I jammed these into my battledress. For some reason I wanted to take the fire axe but couldn't reach it. I had two packs of cigarettes and a pocket full of hard candies. The Lanc was flying well on one engine but was losing height rapidly. My mind was clear and I stood there rehearsing the things I would do as soon as I hit the ground. I felt prepared for anything. Finally the Lanc passed through 500 feet and I knew I had to jump or crash with it, even though I was still over Germany.

"I landed in a shallow pond, only waist deep but ice cold. My parachute ballooned in the wind and it pulled me under the water before I could release it. Oh, God, it was cold! Frozen stiff I stumbled in the dark towards the edge of the pond. I saw a small shack standing on the edge of a railway track with light coming through a crack in the window blind. I made my way to it. My cigarettes and the maps were soaked. My escape kit was still intact, but I gave it little thought. I was freezing to death. I crept up to the shack and looked in. Two railway guards were sitting around a pot-bellied stove. I stood there shivering while I debated whether I should enter but I couldn't think of an alternative. My knees and legs were shaking with the cold. All I wanted was to get warm. All my plans and all my resolve never to be captured vanished and I walked into the hut. The guards jumped up and took me prisoner."

The Bombs That Didn't

Operational flights seldom worked as planned. Often, very often, we made all the preparations, waited nervously all day, and then late at night the trip would be scrubbed. It was usually bad weather that forced the cancellations. It was a bittersweet feeling to be sitting in your bomber, waiting for the time to start engines, only to see a white flare arching into the sky. Once you had climbed aboard you felt committed. After the long dreary day of waiting, the operational briefing, the last supper, dressing, and riding out to the aircraft, you wanted to go. Much of your anxiety was gone and the adrenalin was beginning to flow.

Still, the white flare from the control tower was a reprieve, and if it wasn't too late at night you tried to switch your mind back to more pleasant things. "Wonder if that little redhead will be in the pub, tonight?" Our crew had many trips scrubbed during that fierce winter of 1943, but several weren't caused by weather.

One evening our Lancaster was the last to be bombed and gassed. Aircraft were already taking off and I hadn't started my engines. I sat in the cockpit and fumed as the groundcrew struggled and wrestled with a 4,000 pound bomb, winching it up into the bomb bay. The crew were in position, all I had to do was fire up the engines and go. A tractor under the nose waited to pull the bomb dolly away and the gas bowser was parked in front of the starboard wing, the gas crew frantically topping up the tanks. One of the gas crew was perched on the starboard wing just putting the cap on the last tank. Our target was Berlin. "Christ," I thought, "we're going to be last over the target."

An armourer rushed through the cockpit and into the nose section. I demanded to know what the hell he was doing in here and why the bloody delay. "Just a final check of the distributor switch, skipper, and then it's all set," he called. He began twiddling the knobs and switches that controlled the individual bomb release points.

I turned my attention to the gas crew and sat wondering how long that bastard was going to take before he came off the wing and through the aircraft to the ground. I couldn't start the engines with him out there. My cockpit windows were open and I yelled at him to get weaving.

Bang! The 4,000 pound bomb dropped out of the bomb bay and smashed with a tremendous crash into the tarmac beneath the Lancaster. I froze. Strapped into my seat, my numb brain told me I'd never get through the aircraft and out the back door before the bomb blew up. Staring at the crewman on the wing, I sat frozen with fear as the seconds ticked off. The groundcrew were running in all directions. Slowly I realized the bomb hadn't fused itself and probably wasn't going to explode. It felt like I was part of a slow motion film.

When the crewman had heard the bomb smash down he sprang up and raced along the wing, clearly intending to leap off the end. As he reached the wing tip he hesitated when he realized the distance to the ground, then wheeled and ran towards the fuselage. Nearing the open escape hatch on the roof of the Lanc, his eyes met mine. He stopped and stared. And then he collapsed slowly down on the wing.

I began undoing my seat straps, cursing the bad luck of getting this far into a trip and then not being able to go. Now our crew would have to do another, right from scratch. This one wouldn't count towards the magic thirty. Before I could leave my seat the station commander drove up in his staff car. He parked directly under my cockpit window and climbed out. I could see the gold braid on his cap and the white scarf he always wore as he looked up at me. I wasn't fond of this guy. None of the sergeants were. He seldom flew on a raid, and when he did he had another pilot do the flying. The white scarf was a further irritant.

"You'll not be able to go now, skippah," he shouted up to me. His fake British accent, adopted by so many of our senior officers, made my skin crawl.

"Yeah," I nodded. "You stupid bastard, don't you realize I know that?" But the last comment was under my breath.

It was only a few weeks later that a similar accident occurred on a nearby base, but this time the bombs exploded, blowing up the bomber and killing the crew and several groundcrew.

The long ordeal of preparing for a raid was hard on everyone's nerves. It made you determined that once airborne you were going to get to the target, if at all possible. We were briefed for another raid on Berlin the next day. During the briefing we had been warned that severe icing conditions existed along our route. We probably wouldn't be able to reach 18,000 feet over the enemy coast. We had been programmed over Holland and the Zuider Zee, a heavily defended area ringed with flak guns and searchlights.

The CO said, "If you can't get to 18,000 feet, pick out a few cans of incendiary bombs and drop them to lighten your load."

After a steady climb from base we were at 17,000 feet just ten minutes from the Dutch coast. Flying in solid cloud, with ice building on the wings, the straining Lanc couldn't give us any more height. I had the throttles almost wide open but we hung there almost on the stall. I called Steve and told him to select three cans of incendiaries so we could drop them. Our load consisted of one 4,000 pound blockbuster as well as cans of various sized incendiary stick bombs. Four pounds and thirty pounds each, they were packed into metal canisters. The total bomb load was 6,640 pounds.

Steve, after a long delay, said, "Bomb doors open." I slammed the lever down and heard the roar of the slipstream vibrating the huge bomb doors as I eased the stick forward to maintain speed.

"Bomb doors open," I called.

Whomp. The Lanc jumped, as though lifted by a giant hand, and began to climb rapidly.

"Bombs gone," said Steve, quickly. "Bomb doors closed, skipper."

"Bomb doors closed," I repeated, yanking up the lever. Silence. No one said a word as I set about retrimming the controls. After perhaps five minutes, Eric called on the intercom. "Steve, did the big bomb drop?"

"No, no," replied Steve. "Just the three cans of incendiaries."

"Felt like the big one to me," Stan said.

I said nothing. There was no mistaking when a 4,000 or 8,000 pound bomb left the bomb bay. The Lancaster would literally jump up, the controls becoming light and responsive. The ordeal of the armourer dropping our load in the dispersal had convinced me never to go through the misery of a failed trip again. Besides, if we came home early and said we had dropped our bombs by mistake, we'd never live it down. Far better to face the Germans, bombs or no bombs.

We got to an unbelievable 24,000 feet that night over Berlin. High above the main bomber stream, wobbling along below us at 18,000 to 20,000 feet, we had a ringside seat. I settled into our bomb run on time and track with the aiming flares clearly visible. The city, as usual, was a mass of flame. We could see our bombers silhouetted below, getting hit by flak or with German fighters lacing tracers into them. I felt like an innocent bystander.

"Bomb doors open, skipper," Steve called.

"Roger, bomb doors open."

"Right . . . right . . . steady . . . right . . . steady. Bombs gone." Nothing happened. The Lancaster never jumped.

"Bomb doors closed, skipper."

"Bomb doors closed," I repeated, pulling up the lever. We had just dropped some air over Berlin.

All of the crew knew we hadn't dropped any bombs on the target. Even bomb aimer Steve.

But he would never, never admit it.

Officers All

Bomber Command finally accepted the popular and practical course and agreed that all aircrew should hold commissioned rank. The decision infuriated those pompous pre-war officers who still adhered to rigid concepts of the English class system. Their criterion for an officer and gentleman was nothing less than graduation from an English public school. The RCAF immediately implemented the scheme while the RAF proceeded at a somewhat slower pace.

All aircrew – wireless operators, gunners, flight engineers, bomb aimers, navigators, pilots, the lot – were offered promotion to the rank of Pilot Officer. My objection to accepting a commission unless my gunners were also commissioned was now eliminated.

It was late in February 1944, when I was called to No. 6 Group Headquarters for my commissioning interview with the Air Officer Commanding, Air Vice-Marshal "Black Mike" McEwan. Luckily, the WAAF driver knew the way for my one and only visit to this esteemed headquarters. I had never heard of McEwan, nor had any of my crew, and I wasn't particularly anxious about the interview, one way or the other.

I was shown into a huge office where a giant of a man sat behind a desk some thirty feet from the door. "Sit down," he said. The nearest chair was some twenty feet from his desk, so I sat down in it. McEwan picked a file folder from a pile of papers and without another word to me, began reading through it. I sat there staring at him, until I noticed a small black terrier creep from behind the desk. I called it over to me and waited, playing with his dog, while McEwan read on. After ten minutes he looked up and said, "Was your father in the first war?"

Stunned by the question, I mumbled, "Yes, sir."

"What rank was he?"

"Private."

"What does your father do?"

"He works in a factory."

Silence. After a few minutes McEwan shut the file and said, "You can go."

I left the office wondering what the hell that was all about and who *was* this guy, McEwan. I made it my business to find out, and wished I had done so before the interview. Nicknamed Black Mike for the enormous amount of black hair all over his upper body, he had been an outstanding fighter pilot in World War One, shooting down twenty enemy aircraft.

Shortly after the interview, a signal arrived from Group which said I was now a Pilot Officer. The lowest of the low. I was given £85 and told to buy an officer's uniform. Dutifully, I went to York and got measured for the uniform. After several weeks, I called the tailor to inquire when it would be delivered, only to learn that he had left it in the officers' mess the previous week. After an investigation, it was confirmed that it had been stolen. So I had to wait another two weeks for my first officer's uniform. Meanwhile, they found the officer who had stolen it from the mess, and I had to attend his court martial. This sordid episode confirmed my worst suspicions of officers and officers' messes. But finally I was able to climb into my new costume and hang up my battledress, which I had continued to wear in the sergeants' mess. Now I decided I could properly go to the officers' mess, which at Linton was a pre-war mess and quite elegant for its day.

I showed up one night to check it out, only to discover that I knew none of the aircrew at the bar. They all looked at me and the tiny new ribbon around my sleeve and raised their eyebrows. I could read the message in their eyes. This guy is a sprog officer just over from Canada. The first Canadian woman officer I had seen on the base, a Flight Lieutenant and two ranks my senior, came bustling over to say hello. "You are the first Pilot Officer I've seen in England," she said.

I stood there feeling totally out of place. All of the NCO pilots I had joined the squadron with in June had been commissioned months ago, but all had been shot down. Completely pissed off, a stranger in my own mess, I turned away from the grinning woman and returned to the sergeants' mess and some familiar faces.

With so many aircrew now commissioned, the officers mess was considered overcrowded. The senior officers were hardly able to reach the bar. So they ordered a few Nissen huts bolted together and declared this to be the junior officers' mess. It was so horrible I continued to use the sergeants' mess.

We all thought the commissioning interview a great laugh. Everyone had similar tales to tell. To a man we had been asked, "Was your father in the first war? What rank was he? What does your father do?" To his everlasting credit, one brave soul had replied, "Who in hell is getting this commission? Me or my old man?"

I found out very quickly that being an officer didn't make me a better pilot. On my first raid as a Pilot Officer we went to Essen and got a fierce hammering from the Germans. Obviously those Krauts failed to recognize my new position in life. But in reality, I didn't myself.

When the gunners and I went on our first leave as officers, we suddenly found ourselves in a different category. We were denied entrance to our usual Maple Leaf or Salvation Army hostels and had to stay at commercial hotels. So we went to the "RCAF" hotels, the Regent's Palace and the Strand Palace. We did our drinking at the "RCAF" clubs, the Chez Moi and the Crackers Club, with all the other air force types.

Now that I was an officer, I was expected to have a bank account. No more paybook like the troops. For the vast majority of us, a bank account was a new experience. In the Depression years just past you were lucky if your father had one, let alone you, a kid in school.

London banks were quite impressive structures, and they dealt in leisurely fashion with their regular customers. I looked at them in awe, completely baffled by the intricacies of finance. All of the staff were male and all had rich accents in emulation of the upper class. Pommie accents we called them; rich and fruity. Our pay was sent directly to the bank for deposit and we were never certain if we were overdrawn. I always approached the tellers in trepidation. Would it be possible, I would ask nervously, to get some money? Nothing could have been simpler. It was as though I were entitled to the entire bank.

"Only fifty pounds, sir? Are you quite sure that is sufficient for your leave?"

"But I only have a little more than that in my account."

"Oh, come sir, you mustn't leave yourself short. I really would recommend that you take 100 pounds." Dumbfounded, I would greedily accept the pile of notes. "Now mind, sir, if you should run short, please come in again. Have a nice leave, sir. Good afternoon." It slowly dawned on me that I was considered an officer and a gentleman. A man to be trusted by all English merchants, who foolishly included RCAF officers in that category.

Going to the London tailors was another return to Victorian ways. An English gentleman and his tailor had a relationship that transcended any understanding by colonials. To offer payment, when you ordered a uniform or bought, as they called it, haberdashery, was to offer the tailor an unpardonable insult. You were duly billed in the politest of terms, by a tailor who cherished your custom. You didn't rush in and buy two shirts. You spent a leisurely hour selecting materials and then being measured by at least two tailors for those shirts.

"What would you say, Mr. Smith, a thirty-three and a half sleeve?"

"No, not quite. I would judge slightly less, perhaps thirty-three and five-sixteenths." The two tailors would discuss your measurements in calm, detached tones while you stood in every conceivable position as they measured up, down, and around your arms. The beautiful broadcloth which you selected from various tables was unmatched anywhere in the world. Getting a shirt made to measure has to be a luxury few can afford today, but then it was common practice and one that we sprog officers relished. It wasn't just two shirts, either. A whole dozen, and not a word about filthy lucre.

When one of the largest British tailors, Gieves, was bombed, their records were destroyed in the fire – a catastrophe that would today bankrupt a company that carried so much credit on its books. Not so in those days. Gieves calmly sent every officer in the forces a letter stating that all their records had been destroyed. They wondered if you had an account with them. If so, would you kindly write and tell them the amount you owed. They were terribly sorry to bother you. Amazingly by today's standards, their customers sent along the money.

Some newly commissioned officers never got as far as the tailors. We were all given £85 to buy the first uniform. The equivalent money in Canadian funds in those days was roughly $400. The RAF accounts' officer who counted out those pound notes was a typical money basher, slow and meticulous and devoid of humour. The pound notes were crisp new bills and he had trouble snapping them off, one at a time. Eighty-five for each new officer.

I stood in line waiting my turn at the paymaster's wicket immediately behind Harry Grayson, who was the flight engineer in Hal Miles crew. The accounts' officer eyed Harry with some disdain, as Harry stepped forward and gave his name, Flight Sergeant Grayson. Harry was a character who had been flown home from Sweden in the belly of a Mosquito bomber. His crew had baled out over neutral Sweden when their crippled bomber couldn't make it home. For a long time, Harry's main occupation had been trying to get the goods on his wife back in Canada. He would regale us with stories about the private detective he had hired to spy on her. When he finally got his divorce it had been a wild night in the sergeants' mess. Now he had been made an officer and they were giving him £85. He could hardly believe his luck.

"Eighty-four, eighty-five." With a snap of the last crisp note the paymaster surveyed the pile. It had taken him minutes of slow counting to reach eighty-five, no more, no less. Satisfied, he pushed the pile at Harry.

Grayson lifted the wad of notes and snapped the ends like a deck of cards. *Crack*. "Right on," he said, jamming them into a pocket.

I moved forward for my turn to hear the paymaster mumble, "The man didn't even count them."

Harry immediately went on leave to London wearing his flight sergeant's battledress, and he returned the same way, nine days later.

"How come you didn't buy a uniform?" someone asked him.

"Ran out of money," replied Harry.

Another thing I now had to adjust to was the batman. Every wartime officer had a personal servant to shine his shoes, clean his room, make tea, and keep his wardrobe in shape. Now that so many aircrew were commissioned they ran out of men for these important duties and assigned young WAAF's. However, they were still referred to as batmen for some reason. All were RAF girls, since the Canadian girls had not yet arrived overseas in sufficient numbers. Those who had, worked mainly at RCAF Headquarters in London or the various Group Headquarters.

With so many junior officers and so few batmen we had to share one girl among a dozen officers. One of her important duties was to awaken you each morning. A knock on your door was the signal to come awake. But you were always asked the night before, "What time shall I knock you up in the morning, sir?" When the early morning knock came she would have a cup of tea in her hand. If you played possum she would be forced to open the door and give you a gentle shaking to arouse you. It always did.

Some batmen and their officers became quite chummy and the girl moved into the room, bag and baggage. It worked until the CO found out about it and the officer got the word.

Those who hadn't the courage to use their rooms resorted to the haystacks that dotted the landscape of Yorkshire. Those haystacks became the nesting ground for all amorous Canadians. You always got something if you pedalled off to a haystack with your date, even if only a chance to exchange your bike. The haystack which you thought unoccupied, as you and your girl climbed in, was in reality a seething mass of vibrating humanity. At night it was difficult to see the bicycles surrounding the haystack but once in the stack you realized from the grunts and moans that you weren't alone. The sounds didn't have any effect on the passion of your partner; in fact, it seemed to add to her enthusiasm.

On those nights when you weren't flying it was often raining, and then you sought a less exposed area and headed your bikes towards the transport section. If you happened to be dating a lorry driver it was dead easy. You had access to the wide front seat or, if the lorry was covered by canvas, the entire bed of the truck. It was amazing how many WAAF drivers stowed blankets away in those trucks. With never a word of how it got there, a blanket would materialize.

Occasionally, if the traffic was heavy around the transport section, we would take the long ride out to the aircraft parked around the perimeter of the field. The Lancaster had a rest bed located just behind the main spar. This was a green leather creation, where a wounded crew member could be laid. Not a few crew members got laid there, but most of them weren't wounded.

Don't Look Down

Looking down from the bomb run was often like looking into a blast furnace. Usually a mass of flames, bursting bombs, flak puffs, tracer bullets, shells, flares, and clouds obscured ground features. I can remember seeing only one target clearly during my thirty ops.

Our outward journey that night was fairly routine. When we were over the sea, the gunners asked permission to test their machine guns. The rattle from the eight guns drowned out the engine noise and the reek of cordite wafted up the fuselage. Above, the black sky was hung with huge stars, and Eric used them to check our position by taking star shots with his sextant. When he had finished his calculations he came forward to point out some of the brighter stars in the Big Dipper. He always did this when the sky was clear so I would have an automatic heading in case of a navigation emergency.

The bomb aimer and the pilot both received basic navigation training and could, if necessary, navigate the bomber back to England. But finding our own base, particularly in bad weather, would be terribly difficult. Flying on a star made it easier to jink the aircraft and still maintain a fairly steady course. Jinking meant to pull up forty or fifty feet, roll to the right a few degrees, push down sixty feet, then roll to the left and back near your original height. It was supposed to make it more difficult for the German radar to track you with any accuracy. But too much jinking or weaving made accurate navigation very difficult, even if it did keep the pilot more mentally alert.

I found that flying hour after hour in the dark without a speck of light below and without ever hearing a voice, put me into a reverie. Although I was physically occupied flying the bomber, resetting the compass and monitoring the gauges and flying instruments, the functions were routine and automatic. My mind was free to dwell on a thousand things, even though my eyes searched the darkness ahead. Perhaps it was the brain's method of preventing constant tension; of providing some relief from the awful stress that came from imagining what could happen in the next second. Any communication, no matter how brief, also acted as a diversion. If Eric asked for a change of course, for instance, a map of Europe appeared in my head and I mentally computed our direction and the significance of the change we were making. Stress would ease, too, when the sky was clear enough to note the position of the stars and their relationship to my compass course. I felt more confident that I could navigate the bomber home if the compass was shot away or if Eric was killed. But what if I were killed? Could the rest of the crew get home?

Piloting the aircraft was the weak spot. Only the captain had received pilot training to Wings' standard, although many of the aircrew trades had received some pilot training before being washed out. Once the aircraft was airborne many of them could fly it quite well. But in the majority of cases only the pilot could fly, and since these were the days of only one pilot for each bomber, the aircraft was doomed if the pilot was killed.

As the flight to our target, Stettin, continued, Jock snapped me back to reality by requesting permission to change gas tanks. The engineer controlled the gas switches and electric pumps for transferring fuel and he was supposed to report to me before making a change. It brought into my mind the night he hadn't told me he was changing tanks and had let them drain completely. The air was filled with the screams from four propellers suddenly windmilling at thousands of revolutions per minute as the fuel-starved engines quit. I remembered how terrified I had been at a noise I couldn't identify, and how I had yelled at Jock, seeking a reason.

"It's all reet, skipper," he had said. "I'm just draining the centre tanks." Fuel was always a critical problem, and it was often imperative to get every drop from each tank. I didn't say anything else to Jock, content to let a Scotsman worry about getting every available drop.

As we roared east down the Baltic towards Stettin, I could see hundreds of searchlights reaching into the sky. Confused, I called Eric and told him. "That must be Sweden," Eric said, "we're supposed to cross the southern tip." I thought it odd that neutral Sweden was going to fire at us; but then, as we crossed the Swedish coast, I could see that the flak burst below us. The Swedish guns were laying down a carpet of black and white puffs that turned into a solid layer, so thick it seemed you could walk on it. Not a shell rose above 15,000 feet. I broke silence to call everyone's attention to the ploy. I suppose to those Germans living in Sweden it looked like the Swedes were giving it to us hot and heavy.

As we crossed the German coast the bomber stream turned starboard and headed for Berlin. Often the attack planners would head us towards another city to deceive the German defence system. It forced the Germans to turn on their air raid sirens in many cities and send citizens into the shelters. It was often effective, also, in diverting German night fighters to the wrong areas. It was all part of the intelligence war, each side trying to outwit the other. Mosquito bombers were used for small diversionary attacks on other cities when the main force of heavy bombers was busy elsewhere. During one period that winter a Mosquito was sent to Berlin on thirty consecutive nights. The aircraft was so fast it could outrun the German fighters.

Berlin lay just ahead, outlined by its massive array of searchlights when we swung left and headed north for Stettin. It was a cold and cloudless night and soon we could see Stettin ahead of us, clearly visible in the quarter moon. I could see the Oder River, ice-covered and glinting in the rays of moonlight. We were in the first wave of bombers and as we reached the outskirts of the city the attack had not yet started. The silent scene below looked like a Christmas card. The tiny streets and tiny houses were outlined in sharp relief by a mantle of fresh snow. Just as I wondered if we were too early and would have to orbit the city, the Pathfinder flares exploded in the streets below. We had taken Stettin by surprise. It was four o'clock in the morning.

Heading into our bomb run I could see bombs beginning to burst in the streets, and whole rows of houses erupting skyward as the blockbuster bombs fell among them. We dropped our load squarely on the aiming flares and turned northwest off the target.

As we began the turn, searchlights came on and flak began exploding around us. The flak was too late for us but just in time for the four waves of bombers behind.

It was a strange feeling that crept over me as we began the long flight home. I had been startled to find houses and streets below me as I opened the bomb doors. Everything had looked so peaceful and unprotected – and on a raid I wasn't prepared for anything but danger to myself. As we flew on, I pushed the thoughts of bombs and people from my mind. But I knew I had a new awareness of my job.

Our route home led us back over Sweden's searchlights and heavy flak, with the flak again exploding at 15,000 feet. When we reached the open sea the tension began to ease and I asked Jock to pass me the pee can. The lack of a second pilot made the captain a virtual prisoner, locked in his seat for the entire trip. Few pilots wanted to use the primitive automatic pilot, even when desperate to relieve themselves. The portable toilet (called an Elsan), was perched near the rear door of the bomber. It took a very urgent need to crawl to it through the dark guts of the bomber, especially if flying over enemy territory.

Pilots had their own individual ways of solving part of the problem. I carried a thermos bottle as a relief can, with the glass insides removed for better holding capacity. To use it meant undoing my seat harness, parachute, and Mae West straps and wiggling into a suitable position. Finally, by holding the can between my legs and sitting up as high as possible, I could get some welcome relief. Bombs weren't the only things that burst on a raid.

The first time I used my invention, I motioned to Jock to pass the can to Steve in the nose compartment. I expected Steve to empty it through the chute used to drop "window" and other material. Since Jock and I hadn't spoken on the intercom Steve had no idea of what was in the can, and thinking it was hot coffee he took a swig. I heard about that for weeks.

I thought about that incident as I passed the can to Jock, and Steve came on the intercom to ask, "Are you sure it isn't coffee?" It took my mind back to the days when the squadron was flying Halifax bombers and even more bizarre things happened.

The oldest pilot on the squadron in those days had been a guy everyone called Pop. He loved to drink beer and could handle quite a load. No one in authority worried about drinking and flying. Anyone could belly up to the bar prior to a flight. Only one's self control made the system work. As the raids mounted, Pop's nerves began to fray and he often arrived at his aircraft a mite wobbly. This was always overlooked by his devoted crew as they helped him into the aircraft. On one particular raid, as the story circulated, Pop had climbed aboard with a good snootfull. After an hour in the air he just hauled it out and let fly. Seated below was his Australian wireless operator. Aussie called Pop on the intercom to ask, "Aye say, Pop, is it wrynning out?"

The silence among the crew continued as we flew west over the North Sea. There was an absolute minimum of talking on a raid. Just terse, factual messages were permitted, each essential to the flight. The crew were wired into the intercom system and when a member spoke he turned his microphone switch on only for the time it took to say a few words. Afterwards, he switched it off. Leaving a mike switch open jammed the intercom and prevented anyone else from using it. As the pilot I enforced the practice rigorously, for I was waiting for a yell from a gunner. "Enemy fighter, nine o'clock low, corkscrew port, go!" I didn't want that transmission blocked by an open mike any more than I wanted some ass babbling away about a new girlfriend.

Although the tension of the raid eased as you flew home across the North Sea there was still some danger that a German fighter could be stalking you home. Sometimes they came all the way, letting you lead them into the landing circuit. But as I neared England my thoughts of getting home began to mount as I realized I might actually make it back. Often in my eagerness to sight land I mistook low lying cloud for the coastline. Nothing ever looked as good to me as that first, faint blur of the English coast, low on the horizon in the early pre-dawn light. Then it grew larger, until I could make out a long stretch of land. The bomb aimer strained to pick up a landfall for navigation purposes.

Sometimes I didn't see the coast or our drome until a few hundred feet off the end of the runway. Blind letdowns through heavy cloud and rain, or worse, morning fog, seemed standard procedure. If the base was closed because of weather, they would signal us to divert to another base. Which was okay if we had enough fuel. But the primitive landing instruments in our bombers made every instrument approach a "by guess and by God" arrival.

Many bombers were lost because they couldn't find their base or get down through the atrocious weather. A tired pilot who had wounded aboard or low gas or an aircraft riddled with holes or engines out, had a miserable time trying to find the runway. Bombers crashed all over England. So many, in fact, that the RAF built special airfields near the east coast. Each had a gigantic runway that could handle bombers in emergency situations and was long enough to let a bomber without brakes roll to a safe stop. A system called Fog Investigation Dispersal Operation, (FIDO), was installed on these airfields. Pipes were run the length of the runway, on both sides, and aviation gasoline was pumped through them. The pipes were perforated at intervals, and when the gas was lit, the flames leaped three or four feet in the air, the intense heat dissipating the fog for a height of 100 feet. FIDO saved many a bomber and its crew. Fifteen such airfields were built by the end of the war and 2,400 Allied aircraft made successful landings on them.

The Lancaster had little in the way of landing aids and the pilot felt his radio was really working well if he could be heard for ten miles. The wireless operator had his morse key for wireless messages and could often get a steer to base, but otherwise he was helpless. Flying Control made no attempt, as they do today, to stack the arriving bombers at various altitudes and bring them down one by one. You were simply given a turn to land when you called the tower. "Roger, S Sugar, you are number three to land." So you circled in the cloud and rain with all the others going in any direction that suited.

Coming out of cloud one dark night over Linton, 300 feet above the ground, I emerged directly in the path of another Lancaster. He was coming directly at me and was less than fifty feet from my nose. There wasn't time to think before he roared over the cockpit. Three feet lower and we would have smashed together. All of the crew heard the engines of the other aircraft as it thundered over our heads.

Aircraft with engines shot out had priority for landing, and other aircraft were told to orbit until they landed. Those with two dead engines had immediate priority. The rest of us chased in and out of cloud while the cripples attempted landings.

One dark and miserable morning, a pilot called the control tower just as I was entering the final landing leg. I had the wheels and flaps down when I was told to overshoot. I poured on the power and yanked the wheels up before asking the tower why.

"We have an aircraft on three engines," the controller said. A moment later another voice called the tower asking permission to land. The tower told him, "We have an aircraft on three engines. He has priority."

The pilot came back with, "Well, I've only got two engines."

Immediately the tower gave him number one position, and directed the poor bastard on three engines to stand by. I watched, fascinated, as a Wellington bomber landed. A Wellington aircraft *had* only two engines!

On the night of the Stettin raid, we got back to earth with no particular trouble. I dumped the Lanc onto the runway, and let it roll to the intersection, then began to taxi around the dark perimeter track to our dispersal pad. As I killed the engines, opened the bomb doors, and began shutting off switches, I could hear the groundcrew scuttling around underneath the Lanc. They were looking for hung-up bombs and checking for shell holes, their flashlights bobbing as they checked to see how much work lay ahead.

They were always the same, jocular, sarcastic, irreverent. It was their aircraft and they expected you to treat it right.

"So you got back again?" "Must have been an easy trip – no holes." "What took you so long? Everyone else landed two hours ago." Which was a lie, but their way of saying they'd been waiting all night. They had been waiting. Patiently, in the small shack that served as their tool shed. In the cold and rain and mud and dark. Just as concerned over your safety as you were.

For A Song

The officers' mess was home to all officers, where every officer was equal, regardless of rank. The CO was, of course, afforded certain courtesies and privileges which went with his rank and position. But the junior officer was encouraged to feel that the mess was just as much his home as it was his seniors'. At least this was so on a base where intelligence was not measured by the number of rings on one's sleeve.

It was the junior officers who really made the mess and the more spirited they were, within reason, the more fun for all. Wise CO's knew this, and encouraged a great deal of freedom of expression, though it was an unwritten rule that arguments, fights, or fierce debates were never carried outside the mess. All of this was also characteristic of a peacetime air force – but the wartime officer was a different breed, requiring a somewhat heightened atmosphere. Everyone lived a day at a time with tomorrow blotted out. With each day liable to be your last the behaviour in the mess had a sharply defined quality. It was most evident on party nights, when we all went to the limit of our ingenuity to get the most pleasure from the evening.

The infrequent dance nights presented a certain group of junior officers with the chance to run their favourite contest. They called it the Miss Ugly Contest. The rules were simple. The officer bringing the ugliest woman to the dance won the pooled bets. Each officer anted up £5, approximately $25 in those days, and the pool would be given to the barman for safekeeping. After lunch they would gather at the bar to organize the night's activity and fortify their courage, and after suitable stimulation would head for town. A pub crawl through the seamier sections of the city produced the contestants they were seeking. Just any woman wouldn't do. She had to be not only ugly but thoroughly reprehensible, and her eligibility duly considered and agreed upon by the officers. When all had found his idea of the winner, they crammed into a car and drove to the mess.

They timed their arrival so the dance would be in full swing and the place packed with people. Using a back entrance they smuggled their ladies to the bar and began plying them with large drinks before abandoning them. Stealthily the officers gathered in the games room to decide upon the winner of the pool money. Then in great glee they roared back into town for their own party. Meanwhile, their guests were beginning to mingle happily with the dancers. They had to be seen to be believed. Drunk, dishevelled, stockings hanging down, hair tumbling, some with broken front teeth, some without teeth, dirty, and with beer stained clothes, they lurched onto the dance floor. Some were sick, some were singing, others slipped and fell among the dancers, and some sprawled in all their glory on the mess couches.

It usually took some time in the packed room before the full effect became obvious. Then outraged women descended upon the oblivious CO, demanding that he do something. The embarrassed and livid CO had only one place to vent his fury. On the orderly officer. This unfortunate was instructed in no uncertain terms to get those bloody women out of the mess – now! The poor guy had a hell of a time rounding up and literally dragging the contestants outside to pile them into taxis. The language of the women was rich, even for the air force, as they screamed and yelled that they were invited guests. They demanded to see their boyfriends and wondered who the CO thought he fucking well was, ordering them out?

Contests and bets were constant. Knock rummy was the favourite card game, with poker a close second. Crap shooting, darts, shove ha'penny, and dominoes were other ways of passing time and winning the odd pound note. Bridge was more than a pastime, it was life itself to the fanatics who forever crouched over the cardtables. But there were other diversions. An Australian pilot was the first guy I saw who could drink a beer and eat the glass at the same time. He snapped off pieces of the glass with his front teeth and carefully manoeuvred the pieces with his tongue between his molars. Then he would grind the glass, with a horrible sound, before washing it down with the beer. It was fascinating to see and such a great trick quickly caught on with the more intrepid characters. The novices were "fun" to watch for they always cut themselves and their lips and tongues would bleed. The medical officer would reassure everyone that the glass wouldn't hurt the guy's stomach since it would be dissolved by the stomach acids. But the vast majority of us would rather watch than participate. It was much the same with the guys who staggered back from leave covered in tattoos. While we all gathered to see and hear about them, not many wanted to own any.

Any stranger visiting the mess was set upon at the bar and invited to play the game of the moment. One favourite was, "I'll bet you can't balance a shilling on your nose." Invariably, since it sounded so easy, the victim would accept the bet. Throwing his head back he would put a shilling on his nose, only to have a glass of beer dumped inside his pants.

There were many characters in every mess who fought the war in their own way. One had an imaginary horse that, like the famous rabbit Harvey, accompanied his owner everywhere. Barney called his horse Old Paint. He had a special spot marked out at the bar and woe to the guy who tried to stand there. "You're standing in Paint's place. Can't you see him?" The unwary officer would jump back to collect his wits as Barney ordered another round for Old Paint. This game went on for weeks until it was discovered, on a very drunken night, that Paint had broken a leg and would have to be shot. A gun was duly found and Old Paint was shot and buried behind the bar.

The imaginative owner then turned to other forms of amusement. One that baffled the Flying Control people, and startled many pilots making early morning flights, was his habit of eating breakfast on the end of the runway. He and a friend would rise early and coax the cook to fix them a breakfast, which they then carried out to the very end of the runway. There they would sit, cross-legged, enjoying a leisurely meal. After eating, they left their plates and utensils on the runway and returned to the mess.

Ding Dong Bell was a navigator who somehow managed to complete three tours of operations. An excellent navigator, he was, however, a mite unstable on the ground. You could tell when Ding Dong was around by the stropping sound that accompanied him. He had a huge and wicked looking hunting knife, and a leather strop on which he ceaselessly honed the edge of the blade. Talking to him was difficult because your attention was continually drawn to the knife stropping back and forth. Any unsuspecting arm on the bar or on the edge of a chair was quickly and smoothly denuded of hair in one swift pass with the knife. He was such an eccentric with his wild, staring eyes that he never got challenged. My immediate reaction was a thankful, "God, he could have taken my arm off!" It was wise to keep your sleeves down around Ding Dong. When you did have them rolled up on those rare summer days, you heard a knowing, "I see you've been talking to Ding Dong," as your companion examined your hairless arm. There were others just as zany, and there was seldom an evening without some bizarre event happening. Often from the most unexpected quarter.

I was sitting with three friends at the bar one evening when an Air Commodore came in. For some reason he decided to join our group and introductions were necessary. This guy was tough and rough and had a voice that could break glass at thirty paces. I turned to him and said, "Sir, I'd like you to meet Flying Officers Dingledine, Finklestein, and Finkbeiner."

The Air Commodore let out a roar. "What the hell's going on? Do you think I'm stupid? What are their real names?"

This same commander inspected our entire squadron one day. We were all drawn up in parade ranks in a hangar that had been scrubbed and its aircraft and engine stands removed. It was a full squadron inspection with everyone present: shoes shined, hair cut, uniforms pressed, buttons polished. On such depended the CO's next promotion. There were often a few latecomers to any parade, and this one was no exception. Furtively, a sergeant and a corporal appeared through a side door of the hangar, intent on sneaking into their appointed places unnoticed. As they hesitated, frantically searching for the right file, the Air Commodore arrived with a squealing of tires. The parade was roared into attention. The inspection began.

Resourceful to the last the sergeant dove into one of the large wooden lockers that lined the walls of the hangar. The corporal, not to be outdone, dove into the locker next to him. When the formal inspection had finished, the Air Commodore asked to see the squadron offices and workshops. Blithely unaware of the two NCO's hiding in the lockers, the CO led the Air Commodore on a tour of inspection, explaining how the squadron operated and pointing out things of interest that would show efficiency. Passing the lockers, the Air Commodore paused for a moment to inquire why they were so large. "They are used to store the airmen's tool kits as well as their clothes, sir," explained the CO. "They are quite useful, sir."

"I see," said the Air Commodore, grasping the handle of a locker and flinging it open. There stood the sergeant, stiffly at attention. The Air Commodore never batted an eye. "I suppose," he snapped, "that if I opened this one," and he indicated the next locker, "a bloody corporal would be in here." He yanked open the door, took a look at the corporal standing frozen with fear, and slammed the door shut. "Just as I thought," he said.

Fear of death – not just fear of being late – was so strong in some of the aircrew that no form of discipline was effective. These were the ones who had convinced themselves they would be killed and everything else was therefore trivial. Joe was one of those, and he became the mess drunk. Rarely washing or shaving he slept in his clothes, caring only for the next beer. Everyone tried to avoid him, for we had long since stopped trying to help. Often Joe would get so drunk he would be unable to get back to barracks, and he would curl up on a couch for the night. His end came on the morning the CO and some senior officers inspected the mess to make arrangements for the arrival of some politicians. The CO and his group were standing in the ante-room discussing how the reception should be handled when a booming fart burst from a couch. The startled officers and a furious CO turned to look. A bleary-eyed, unshaven face appeared over the back of a couch. Staring at the CO in triumph, Joe said, "No fucking Group Captain could do that." Joe disappeared from the base that very morning.

There were several kinds of parties held by a squadron. When a crew completed thirty operational trips they were screened, and a wild party followed, often lasting for days. Usually the lucky crew would take over a pub and invite their groundcrew to join in the festivities.

When a squadron was stood down from operations, the entire squadron celebrated. A hangar would be cleared for an all-ranks bash that continued until morning or until the kegs of beer had been drained, events which often coincided. These were all-out, no-holds-barred drunks that gave everyone a chance to blow off steam. If you had a CO like Tiny Ferris, the party was great, for he led the highjinks and drank the most beer. If the CO was rank-hungry and aloof, the party never got off the ground. But there were other kinds of parties, and perhaps the zaniest were those in the various messes. They were modelled on RAF traditions, which the RCAF had adopted, modified, and in some respects improved upon. The age group being what it was, the humour was of the high-school variety. The idea of removing a guy's pants seemed hilarious fun, especially if they were the CO's pants.

Dining-in nights at the messes were infrequent in wartime, but they held to the usual pattern, which called for a very formal dinner. After dinner the bar and the piano became the entertainment centres. After considerable fortification, the games would start. Off with the CO's pants, if he could be captured, but it was more often some unsuspecting sprog, newly arrived, who was denuded. Corks would be burned and the sooty black cork smeared on the bare buttocks of the struggling victim. When his ass was thoroughly blackened, willing hands raised him into a doubled position and he would be rammed against the walls of the mess. Often his testicles would be included in the imprint. As the party got into high gear more daring feats were attempted. A crowd would support a guy whose feet had been blackened with the burnt cork while he walked up a wall, across the ceiling, and down the other side. The black footprints looked weird but not half as weird as they appeared the next day.

Meanwhile, others were engaged in beer drinking contests. Formed into teams, each had to down his pewter mug of beer in sequence, then place the empty mug upside down on his head. First team to have all their mugs on their heads won the game. The contest never went according to the rules. Mugs would be filled with strange concoctions while the unwary player was diverted.

A game called chesterfields was supposed to represent an army tank battle. Two teams were chosen and positioned at the ends of a long room. At the command from the CO to charge, they hoisted huge leather couches on their shoulders and ran towards each other. Bodies and broken furniture flew in all directions.

The RCAF had added their own games to the RAF's repertoire, and buck-buck was one of the crazier innovations. It appealed to the big, outdoor types who loved to play rugger or football. Two teams of eight were chosen or commandeered since the CO was the referee and his invitation to play was difficult to refuse.

A flip of the coin decided which team would be first on the

defensive. The team captain would stand, back against the wall, facing the room. His team would then form into a single file facing him, each bent over and clutching the man in front of him around the thighs. Their backs then formed a landing field for the other team who, in turn, ran and vaulted onto the bent-over backs. When all the offensive players had leaped onto the line, the last man to land would hold up several fingers and call, "Buck-buck, how many fingers do I have up?" If the other team guessed correctly they became the jumpers. The odds against guessing correctly doomed the bent-over figures to more torture as the game continued with increased ferocity. If the line collapsed from the weight of bodies, the other team had the right to continue jumping. After two or three unsuccessful attempts to hold their own, the bent-over players began to devise ways to slow their opponents' vigour. At a whispered command the whole line would shift sideways just as an opponent was airborne. As the victim crashed on the floor a howl of protest rose from the cheering section.

Ears were ripped, knees permanently injured, ribs broken, noses squashed, eyes blackened, and clothes torn, but no one seemed to notice during the heat of battle. Eventually the game got so rough, and so many injuries were inflicted, that buck-buck was outlawed from our squadron.

One or two distinguished visitors were usually invited to the dining-in nights. They were politicians or senior government officials or serving officers from one of the other services. We had two RCMP senior officers attend one night as guests of the CO. Adorned in their official mess dress, complete with jodhpurs, riding boots, and spurs, they looked very dashing and every inch the epitome of constabulary correctness. Each had a small pencil-thin mustache and straight black hair, greased flat across the head with not a trace of sideburns; they looked very prim and proper.

As our games got more frantic the two RCMP types stood against the bar, brandies in hand, looks of disdain flickering over their sharp features. You could read their minds: "bloody foolish nonsense." The CO was anxious that his guests take part in the games and tried unsuccessfully to get them involved. They politely declined all invitations.

When someone shouted blind-man's-buff, a roar went up and a

mob descended upon the bar, surrounding the two RCMP officers. The CO got the message immediately. The squadron wanted new blood. Turning to the officer guests he invited them to try this game, explaining how simple it was and how much fun. "Two men are blindfolded and seated on the floor facing each other. Each has a rolled up magazine and they take turns trying to hit the other fellow. It's bags of fun and harder than it looks when you're blindfolded. You must try it."

"Well, no, really," they both smiled politely. "We don't think so."

"Oh, come on," the CO implored, "you must have a go. It only takes a few minutes."

"No," they both rhymed, "we'd rather watch, if you don't mind."

"Tell you what I'll do," said the CO. "If one of you chaps will play against one of my men, you can have the first wallop." The thought of delivering the first blow was too much for one of the policemen, and his eyes sparkled as he grabbed the bait.

"You're sure I get the first blow?"

"Absolutely, I'm the referee and it's guaranteed," said the CO.

Convinced, the RCMP officer got slowly down on the floor as the crowd moved back. He lowered himself carefully into a sitting position, adjusted his jodhpurs, his feet spread wide and his spurs turned outwards, and tugged down his tunic. The CO handed him a large magazine and he spent a few moments rolling it into a tight roll and thumping it into his other hand, to test its strength. A young pilot got down on the floor opposite him and took a rolled newspaper for his weapon. Meanwhile, the CO tied a large serviette around the RCMP officer's head and over his eyes.

"Can you see?"

"No," replied the officer.

"You're sure everything's okay?" the CO queried.

"Yes, I'm ready," the officer smiled broadly, "tell me when to start."

Immediately, his opponent stood up and moved back. The rest of the action was a blur as two large mugs of beer were poured between the RCMP officer's legs and eager hands grabbed his feet and pulled him forward into the puddle of beer.

The mess erupted in screams of laughter as the victim snatched off his blindfold to discover how he had wet his jodhpurs. Even the other RCMP officer snickered as he watched his buddy rise slowly from the floor, his crotch dripping beer, his dignity dead.

As the evening wore on, the party broke into groups, some playing cards, others shooting craps on the billiard table; but the majority gathered around the piano, roaring out the air force songs.

Many of the songs we sang borrowed their lyrics from popular songs of the day, especially the bawdy music-hall numbers. Everyone knew the tunes, even if they couldn't remember the words. Some songs originated in a period before the Crimean War. Others had been sung in World War One, and some were born in military outposts between the wars. Many that we sang were copied from army and navy favourites, with RAF words substituted. There seemed to be several versions of each song, which often was the result of a newly arrived musical genius on the squadron. What they had in common was the foul language of the work-a-day air force, language born out of loneliness, frustration, and fear. The vulgarity opened an avenue for the pent-up hostility each airman harboured against an official service that had stationed him in some ghastly hole, halfway round the world. Why did we sing? Helpless to control our lives, we turned to song to express the insanities of the moment. We were lonely, homesick, frightened, powerless, and as one of the songs so aptly expressed it, "There's fuck all else to do."

Any sing-song also included recitations. Some were solo renditions, others demanded a question and answer format. If you didn't know the words, no matter; you knew the chorus which was repeated and repeated. But it didn't take long before you caught them, even if you didn't understand them all.

Sing a song or buy the beer was a popular custom. Those songs went on and on, verse after verse held together by the ribald chorus as each in turn had to sing a verse or buy the beer for the crowd. Improvisation happened on the spot as the wary singer frantically thought up words to satisfy the yelling crowd. Any old rhyme was permissible if it was funny and in keeping with the bawdy mood.

The sing-song would begin with RAF versions of old army songs like "The Quarter Master's Stores," but with the words changed to reflect RAF life.

148

There was flak, flak, bags of bloody flak,
In the Ruhr, in the Ruhr.
There was flak, flak, bags of bloody flak,
In the Valley of the Ruhr.

And then the chorus which followed each verse:

My eyes are dim I cannot see,
The searchlights they have blinded me.
The searchlights they have blinded me.

"Bless 'Em All" was a song from the navy, and it, too, had been changed to suit RAF conditions.

They say there's a Lancaster
Just leaving the Ruhr
Bound for old Blighty's shore
Heavily laden with flak frightened crew
Scared stiff and prone on the floor.

Then the chorus:

You'll get no promotion this side of the ocean
So cheer up my lads, fuck 'em all.

Every squadron seemed to have at least one Australian flyer, and he would have to sing "Waltzing Matilda." When the clean version was finished, the crowd would call for "Ops In A Wimpey," which was sung to the same tune.

Ops in a Wimpey, ops in a Wimpey,
Who'll come on ops in a Wimpey with me?

One of the songs sung by all three services had started in the army in World War One; "Where Are The Boys Of The Old Brigade?"

I don't want to be a soldier,
I don't want to go to war,
I'd rather hang around Piccadilly Underground,
Living off the earnings of a high born lady.

I don't want a bullet up me arsehole
I don't want me bollocks shot away,
I'd rather stay in England, Merry, Merry, England
Rogering me bleedin' life away.

There were many verses, and one of the more popular ones, as I recall, went like this:

Send out the Boys of the Old Brigade,
That set old England free,
Send out my brother, my sister and my mother,
But for Christ's sake, don't send me.

There were some songs to which everyone knew the words, partly because they were sung so often, and partly because they had such great appeal for the airmen. "O'Reilly's Daughter" was the one our squadron loved.

As I was sitting by the fire,
Drinking Reilly's rum and water,
I was taken by desire
To go and shag O'Reilly's daughter.

Now up the stairs and into bed,
There I threw my right leg over,
She didn't mind a goddamn bit,
She laughed like hell when the shag was over.

As I was coming down the stairs,
Who should I meet but the one-eyed Reilly,
With two pistols in his hands,
Looking for the man who shagged his daughter.

There were also many recitations that involved conversations between cockneys, perhaps because of the attractive accent. Anyone who could mimic the accent was pressured into this one. It's a conversation held by two cockney women over the backyard fence.

I'll tell you Mrs. Higgins, Lobsters might be good for you, and Oysters will go straight to a man's balls, but Shy-rimps, Christ, is they powerful.

150

The other night me Harry comes home from the pub where he's
had his beer and pint of Shy-rimps and he climbs in bed with
me.
Can I borrow your thing for a minute love? he asks.
Nar, Harry, I says, get to sleep.
And before you can say Trafalgar Square, there's half a noggin
of his nasty nature all over the ceiling.
And wot with the drip, drip, drip, all night long I never got a
wink of sleep.
I'll tell you Mrs. Higgins, Lobsters might be good for you, and
Oysters will go straight to a man's balls, but Shy-rimps, Christ,
is they powerful!

"Somersetshire" was a song that came out of the desert bases
manned by the RAF during the wars. The song was named for the
troop ship, *Somersetshire,* that transported the airmen back and
forth to England. New verses were added to keep abreast of cur-
rent events.

O Shire, Shire, Somersetshire,
The skipper looks on her with pride.
He'd have a blue fit, if he saw all the shit,
On the side of the Somersetshire.

This is my story, this is my song,
We've been in the air force too fucking long,
So roll on the Nelson, the Rodney, Renown,
You can't sink the Hood, for the bastard's gone down.

The common phrase for a party was a "knees up," which came
from a song called "Knees Up Mother Brown."

Oh, knees up, Mother Brown,
Knees up, Mother Brown.
Come along dearie, let it go,
E-I-E-I-E-I-O
It's your bloomin' birthday,
Let's wake up all the town,
So, knees up, knees up,
Don't let the breeze up,
Knees up, Mother Brown.

And no party sing-song was complete without the popular "Salome."

Down our street there was a merry party,
Everyone there, oh so gay and hearty,
Talk about a treat, we ate up all the meat,
And we drank up all the beer from the boozer down the street.

There was old Uncle Ted, he was fair fucked up.
Down in the cellar with the old bull pup,
Little sonny Jim trying to get it in,
With his arsehole winking at the moonlight.

Oh, Salome, Salome, that's my girl Salome,
Standing there with her arse all bare,
Every little wrinkle makes the boys all stare.

She's a big fat cow, twice the size of me,
With hairs on her ass like the branches of a tree.
She can run, jump, fight, fuck,
Wheel a barrow, drive a truck,
That's my girl Salome.

Jesus wants me for a sunbeam,
And a fucking good sunbeam, I'll be.

The song "John Peel" was corrupted a dozen ways. There were countless verses, some composed on the spot.

The donkey is a solitary moke,
He very seldom gets a poke,
But when he does, he lets it soak,
As he revels in the joys of copulation.

The chorus went like this:

Cats on the roof tops, cats on the tiles,
Cats with syphilis, cats with piles,
Cats with their assholes wreathed in smiles,
As they revel in the joys of copulation.

Usually the sing-song ended on the long-drawn-out verses of "That Was A Cute Little Rhyme."

That was a cute little rhyme,
Sing us another one
Just like the other one
Sing us another one, do.

There was a young plumber from Dee
Who was plumbing his girl by the sea,
Said the girl, stop your plumbing,
For I hear someone coming,
Said the plumber, still plumbing, it's me.

There was a girl named Gail,
Between her tits was the price of her tail,
And on her behind, for the sake of the blind,
The same information in Braille.

There once was a man named Skinner,
Who took a young girl out to dinner,
At quarter to nine they sat down to dine,
At quarter to ten, it was in her.
No, not the dinner, but Skinner.

There was a young queer from Khartoum,
Who took a young friend to his room,
They argued all night, over who had the right
To do what and with which and to whom.

There was a young man from Dundee,
Who buggered an ape in a tree,
The result was most horrid, all ass and no forehead,
Three balls and a purple goatee.

The sing-song would finally wear itself out as people went to bed – or tried to, until waterfights brought them alive again. Flares were shoved into fireplaces or down chimneys, the kitchen was raided, fire alarms pulled, and bicycle races careened around the mess.

Wizard party!

"Press On, Regardless"

As the harsh winter of 1943-44 deepened and the Battle of Berlin went on endlessly, we lost more and more crews. I began to wonder if I would survive my tour.

The squadron was detailed for a raid on Leipzig on February 19. Leipzig lies ninety miles southwest of Berlin and some seventy-five miles from the Czechoslovakian border. A long stooge of seven and a half hours for the Lancaster, yet only 2,300 direct air miles. The trouble was that we couldn't fly directly to the target, but had to detour hundreds of miles to avoid the heavier defence zones. This made for maximum gas loads and, consequently, fewer bombs, which Harris and his planners didn't like. Orders were issued to remove the armour plating and to reduce the amount of ammunition carried in order to save weight and thus increase the bomb load. Even the rest bed was ordered removed. The aircrew all bitched and protested but to no avail.

To reach Leipzig we were routed east over Holland and the Zuider Zee, south of Bremen, north of Hanover, and between Berlin and Magdeburg, then south to Leipzig. The route home was almost due west, in an attempt to stay south of the Ruhr Valley and north of the Rhine Valley. With our primitive navigation instruments and the lack of reliable winds, the navigator's job was made extremely difficult. The weather on that raid was foul, with terribly high winds that blew many bombers off course and over heavily defended cities.

Seventy-two aircraft failed to return from Leipzig, which was 10 per cent of the raiding force. Our squadron lost four crews on that raid to add to the six crews lost in January. Our sister squadron, No. 426, was suffering similar losses. On January 27 we lost three crews over Berlin, and 426 squadron lost four crews. The total losses made noticeable differences on the base. Our friends were disappearing at an alarming rate. New crews arrived and went missing before you had the chance to know them. They were merely names chalked on the order-of-battle board in the operations room; names erased and replaced each day.

The four crews shot down over Leipzig were all new crews. One was on its very first raid. Another was doing its second trip, and the other two were doing their third and fourth trips. Twenty-eight men disappeared from the mess. Losses of 25 per cent made you stop and think. It also gave me the idea that experience was the answer, and with twenty-six raids under my belt I felt experienced. Until the next night, when Bob Smith was shot down on his twenty-first trip. So much for experience.

A full complement of crews was twenty per squadron, and we lost exactly twenty crews in the first three months of 1944. February was the worst month in the history of the squadron when eight crews went down in the most horrible flying weather imaginable. The month was a nightmare. Three times as many trips were scrubbed as flown, and day after day it was a constant round of briefing, standby, scrubbed; briefing, standby, scrubbed. You could cut the tension that gripped the squadron with a very dull knife.

When I look back on those casualty figures today it seems incredible that I survived, but at the time I never measured the odds. I had an unshakable belief that I was invincible; that our crew was the best in Bomber Command and no German could possibly shoot us down. Such faith belongs to the young and without it, I suppose, few would have flown. Viewed today it smacks of arrogance, conceit, and stupidity. I can only admit that as I flew more and more raids, I grew contemptuous of the danger.

Each raid had a cumulative effect. Each added its own particular terror to the preceding ones, which you carried forward until you felt you had seen and experienced all of the horrors the night sky could fling at you. It built an unconscious esteem, a pride of self, that arose from surmounting the difficulties of the job. Not everyone thought he was invincible; rather the opposite. The more intelligent aircrew simply pointed to the statistics and drew the obvious conclusion.

In the quiet moments, there were many theories expressed

among the aircrew on how to survive a tour. Who would be killed and who would survive and why. But they were mere conjectures. The answer to what made a successful crew has never been established, as it never can be with so many horrible factors to consider. Luck certainly played a major role, as it does in any military action, and this was proven time after time.

Losses were announced by the BBC. We called the nightly radio news broadcasts the voice of doom, and the mess would hush for the ten o'clock report.

"Last night bombers of the Royal Air Force attacked Berlin, dropping 2,500 tons of bombs. Crews reported extensive damage and huge fires were visible for 150 miles. Sixty-five of our bombers failed to return."

Never a mention of the RCAF; that we had taken part. It produced a howl of protest from the enraged Canadians. Except for that nightly newscast we would never have known how many crews were lost. We knew our own squadron losses only because we were part of the action. No. 6 Group aggregate losses were never announced in any form.

It was hard to find squadron commanders who could boost morale, and Tiny Ferris had left a large pair of shoes. The squadron spirit developed by Ferris, and brought to its peak during our transition from Halifax to Lancaster, was now gone. The third CO in less than a year was trying to get us motivated, but he was to be shot down in a few months.

In essence, the job was too big for the average officer. Bomber Harris and his group commanders were biting off more than they could chew in attempting to destroy Berlin; to make it another Hamburg. The route to the Holy City was long and difficult, almost as far as the Lancaster could reach. In addition, Berlin was the most heavily defended target in Germany, and the weather that winter was atrocious. The weather hindered our operations almost as much as the Germans. Churchill made it clear to Harris that he didn't expect Bomber Command to have to fight the weather as well as the enemy. But in truth, Harris had little choice. He was also too stubborn to admit any difficulty in his fanatical zeal to bring Germany down. Any commander who showed the least hesitation, or who questioned his wisdom, suffered his total contempt.

If Harris had made just one raid and watched what was happening over the North Sea, he might have been persuaded to change his mind. It was the quickest way of judging the terrific strain on the aircrew. Common practice called for a bomber to jettison its bombs into the sea if mechanical problems occurred. You were instructed not to return and attempt a hazardous landing with bombs on board. When you saw bombs exploding and photo flashes streaking the sky, you knew someone had lost an engine or his oxygen system had failed or some other fault had occurred, and the bomber was aborting the trip. On any given night perhaps a dozen flashes would be visible from your position in the bomber stream. But as that interminable Battle of Berlin raged, the flashes over the sea grew more frequent and less attributable to mechanical fault. It looked, on some nights, as though the entire force had been recalled; as though everyone was jettisoning his bombs and turning back.

"Ray," I would call our wireless operator, "are you sure there hasn't been a general recall?"

"No, skipper, I've been listening out the whole time. What's the problem?"

"Take a look outside. Every bastard and his brother is jettisoning his bombs. They're all going home. We're the only crew left."

To see over 100 of those flashes convinced you that you were the only crew going on to the target.

Bomber Command finally got so concerned by these early returns that they ordered the automatic camera to be hooked to the release wire of the big bomb. The camera was used to take target photos but if your bombs landed on the target it was rare to obtain a clear picture. It was entirely possible, however, to get a photo over the sea. Now, when the crews jettisoned their bombs into the sea, the camera recorded exactly where they dropped. Some crews persisted in evading by other means. Some were discovered droning north and south over the sea, waiting until it was time to land back at base. Unfortunately, they forgot that the RAF radar stations were watching.

The climate of trust that had marked our earlier operations vanished, and the interrogations after a raid turned bitter as accusations were flung at the crews. Each debriefing now became an inquisition as the staff officers, station commander, and squadron commanders demanded explanations of everything. To be exposed to such a grilling was a bitter experience that your pride had difficulty accepting.

Once I returned early because all my flying instruments had frozen. This was always a problem in the Lancaster and it happened several times with S Sugar. The problem lay in the static vent that governed the airspeed indicator. The long copper line that ran from the pitot tube in the nose of the bomber back to the rear door and connected to the static air vent would gather moisture when the aircraft was parked in dispersal. Your flying instruments acted normally until you flew above the freezing level. Then the water in the line froze, blocking the air, and you were left without altimeter, airspeed indicator, or rate of climb indicator. It was difficult enough to navigate with everything working, but it was impossible without knowing your speed and height. When I gave the reason for my early return, the CO gave me a tremendous blast. He told me I had no right to return over such a simple thing.

"Why didn't you press on to the target?"

I gave him the reasons and added that I wasn't trying to win the Victoria Cross. But his implication that I had been too chicken to continue the trip stung all of the crew, and left me wondering what kind of brains were needed to be a CO.

It wasn't really the CO's fault, for he was under considerable pressure from No. 6 Group Headquarters and Bomber Command Headquarters. Anything less than a maximum effort was considered his responsibility and a failure to instill the proper fighting spirit. Crews were exhorted to press on when an engine failed, which was entirely possible on the shorter routes, such as those to the Ruhr Valley, but not on the long stooges to Berlin, Leipzig, or Munich. A crippled bomber couldn't keep up with the main stream and fell too far behind and too low, a sitting duck for the German fighters. Nevertheless, we were badgered and openly threatened to continue at any cost, and "Press on, regardless" became a stock joke among the crews.

On one occasion, one of our crews who returned early reported they had lost an engine as they started to cross the English Channel. Not giving the captain a chance to explain, the CO thundered at him. "Why didn't you press on? You still had three good engines."

"I told you," said the sergeant pilot, "we lost an engine."

"You could have made it on three engines. You had no business turning back."

"You don't understand," the exasperated pilot yelled. "The engine didn't just quit. The whole fucking thing fell off the wing! We were damn lucky to fly it home."

Faced with what they considered impossible odds, many aircrew simply quit. It was rare for an entire crew to quit but nearly every crew had one member pack it in. Panic-stricken lest the refusal to fly became endemic, Bomber Command reacted with ferocious cruelty against these unfortunates. Each was immediately stripped of his rank and banished overnight to an Aircrew Refresher Training Centre. In reality this was a punishment camp where the kid's spirit was destroyed. Everyone who had the courage to march into the CO's office and say, "That's it. I quit. I can't fly anymore," was branded with the tag, Lack of Moral Fibre or LMF as it was universally known. This was the most loathsome expression the RAF could find for a man who had, to them, failed in the face of the enemy. To the everlasting shame of the RCAF, this stupid and inhuman practice was adopted without hesitation and was applied with great vigour that winter. Despite the stigma and the immediate, horrible consequences, a kid who could no longer force himself into his bomber simply said, "I will not fly again, no matter what you do to me."

Non-commissioned aircrew were easily handled, but officers presented a more difficult problem. They had access to court martial proceedings and the attendant publicity which the authorities disliked. Usually they were quietly returned to Canada as quickly as possible. The reaction of the crews to this LMF system was one of disdain and disgust, and it eroded any last bit of respect we might have felt for the leadership of our group. Our position was simply, "There but for the grace of God go I."

Had a crew member refused to fly on his first trip, rather than on his fifth or tenth or even twentieth raid, perhaps it would have been easier to apply the label. But to have tried and tried valiantly and then been unable to do the prescribed thirty trips was not, in any sense of the word, cowardice.

I lost two crew members who could not continue to fly operations any longer. One was Ray, our wireless operator, who baled out on his sixth trip, preferring prisoner of war confinement to the known horrors of flying ops. The other, Harry, our flight engineer, couldn't continue past seven trips and decided to ground himself. All of our crew were concerned, but no one was critical or anything but sympathetic and understanding. Both Ray and Harry had worked hard, and I considered them very capable airmen, but they simply couldn't endure the strain of operational flying. Nothing difficult to understand. Nothing dishonourable in my eyes. They had certainly tried. The mistake, if one was made, lay with the initial aircrew standards board that had selected them for flying duties.

The fear of flying operations was a constant with most aircrew. It had to be. My own fear was easier to carry because I was captain of the aircraft, young enough to accept all the guff we had been brought up to believe. "The captain always goes down with the ship," and other fairy tales. I might be terrified – but I mustn't let my fear be known to my crew.

One evening, over some beers, Eric asked, "Why do you swear so much when we get into trouble over Germany?"

I was completely stunned by his question. "Swear? You're kidding!"

"No, really, every time we get caught in the searchlights or get hit by flak or have a fighter up our ass, you start cursing."

I found his remarks hard to believe and I sat there conscious that I was afraid to examine the question. "Maybe," I said, in an attempt to change the subject, "it's because I love those bastards so much." But I made a mental note to check it out. Sure enough, Eric was right. Whenever we got into a tangle with the enemy and I began throwing the bomber around, trying to get away, I found myself cursing the Germans. "You rotten bunch of bastards. You sneaking, yellow sons of bitches." I kept it up until we got free.

While Eric recognized my behaviour patterns, I don't think he knew his own. He would throw up before boarding the bomber for each operational trip. Never on training flights, just on ops. One moment he was standing with the crew waiting for the time to board, and the next minute he was bent over the tail wheel vomiting. His hands shook continually, and since he was a small kid, very pale and blond, he looked like a nervous, fluttering chicken. He never mentioned his obvious nervousness, neither did the crew. Once in the air he was efficiency itself, keeping the aircraft on track and on time. We never failed to find the target or base on return. I thought he was the greatest and so did the crew. Eric compounded his reasons for nervousness by marrying a lovely English girl when we were halfway through our operational tour. He then had more than himself to worry about.

The operational word for nerves was the twitch. You could see it at the bar anytime. Facial muscles would twitch involuntarily without the owner's awareness. Some of the guys were funny to watch and I always stood next to the guy with the most pronounced twitch. Some would flutter an eye, some would stutter slightly as their mouths jumped around. Some had a jerky arm or leg that would twist and leap. When two or three guys with a decent twitch got together it was a hilarious sight. One senior officer would begin to speak and after about six words his jaws would lock open. His eyes bulged out and he would gurgle and gargle trying to speak. It was funny to see; but not so funny when you were standing in front of his desk, desperately trying to understand the order he was fighting to deliver. These manifestations of the stress caused by operational flying were always understood and allowed for by other aircrew. It was, in effect, a badge of honour.

Each flyer had his own particular fear. Some, like myself, dreaded the searchlights. Some hated the German fighters. Some even hated flying. I didn't fear the fighters, figuring naively, that I could handle a one-on-one situation. Bob Young, who came from Niagara Falls, would tease me constantly about how I would meet my end. "A night fighter will get you for sure." Unfortunately, it was a night fighter that got Bob during a raid on Düsseldorf. When he failed to return I began to think more seriously about the fighters. But in truth, it was the bloody searchlights that terrified me. It wasn't until my third Berlin raid that I met my personal fear face to face.

I had just settled the Lanc into a straight and level bombing run, bomb doors open and vibrating as I followed the course directions of the bomb aimer. Berlin was sixty miles of flame, smoke, bursting shells and bombs, and, it seemed, millions of glaring searchlights sweeping the sky. I could spot dozens of bombers below, converging on the Pathfinder flares, some already in flames and plunging down. I held the Lanc steady as Steve dropped our bombs, every nerve in my body screaming to turn off the target and flee this inferno. I had just closed the bomb doors when I went blind. Absolutely blind. Terrified, I realized we had been coned. The world was a dazzling white, as though a giant flashlight was aimed directly into my eyes.

I couldn't see my hands on the control column, couldn't see the instrument panel, couldn't see outside the cockpit. I was naked, totally exposed, helpless. Foolishly I told the gunners to keep searching for fighters, but they were as blind in their turrets as I was in the cockpit. I could tell the flak hadn't started up the beams because we weren't being rocked by bursts. That meant the search-lights were illuminating us for fighter attacks. Paralyzed with fear, I tried to get my brain working. I had seen enough bombers coned by searchlights to know it was useless to turn and twist hoping to break out of them. We were a very bright and shiny target in the apex of fifty or more beams that were radar directed. They weren't going to let go easily.

Instinctively I reacted by shoving the nose down hard and jamming the throttles forward. My brain was screaming at me: the shortest distance between two points is a straight line. Dive. Out-run the lights. My speed built up rapidly as I hurtled down, the controls stiffening. I had no idea of my direction or even if I was turning. I tried to keep the controls centred. Cupping my hands around the airspeed indicator to block the light, my chest holding the control column forward, I got a reading of 350 miles an hour. The altimeter needle was whirling backwards so fast my panicky brain failed to register a reading. Fearful that I would fly us into the ground I began easing back on the stick. I was covered in sweat and trembling with fear. In my mind's-eye I could see fighters rac-ing in for the kill. The Lanc roared over the blazing city and after an eternity, finally out-distanced the lights.

Bang. The window in the nose was blown out by a burst of flak that peppered the fuselage and engines. A howling wind blew maps and charts and dust into the cockpit, as Steve tried desperately to block the hole. Abandoning the hopeless task, he crawled back to the navigation section. We were now below 4,000 feet and I asked Eric for a safety height. He told me to climb to 20,000 feet and we began the long trek home, frozen by the frigid air blasting in through the nose.

Eric later estimated that we had been coned by sixty search-lights. It seemed more like 250 to me. He had, amazingly, timed how long we had been held by the lights. Seven minutes. Only a navigator thinks like that.

Now, at last, I had confirmed that my fear of searchlights wasn't totally irrational. Each light was more than two million candle power. Not all beams were radar controlled, usually only the master beam, which was so white it had a bluish tinge. It did the job of illuminating the bomber. Then the manually operated slave beams clustered together on the aircraft. Going into Ruhr Valley targets, the lights stretched for endless miles, from city to city. You could be coned by lights from cities you weren't attacking. Often a bomber flying beside you would be coned. It would twist and turn, with the flak streaming up to it, and you would pray that the lights held it long enough for you to creep safely past.

I was never able to overcome my fear of the lights. On practice raids over English cities I would deliberately fly into masses of searchlights, hoping to find some sure way to escape. I had Ken, in the mid-upper turret, concentrate on the wings to see if he could tell when they were level with the horizon. But none of our experiments worked and I found I was just as terrified whether they were English or German searchlights. My fear, however, did make me more sympathetic towards those who could not continue to fly.

The harsh treatment they received sickened me. Had our commanders shown any compassion or tried in any way to rehabilitate them, they could have continued flying. Professional medical advice was ignored and psychiatric help scorned. The service view held that they must be punished. Anything less would be an admission of leniency, and any such tolerance would be bad for the service. Particularly so for the CO, who would be considered something less than enthusiastic, and relieved of his command. The promotion of a CO depended upon a well-run, efficient unit with good morale. He wasn't going to admit a problem existed.

In truth, a bomber squadron was terribly difficult to lead. Unlike the fighter commander, the bomber CO could not be seen to lead in the air. He flew at night, removed from his squadron, without even radio contact, an entity like everyone else in the great bomber stream. The crews had no way of judging his operational ability. Yet some CO's had great success in building a strong, spirited squadron. In every case this was done by strength of personality; the willingness to take all the risks their crews endured. The successful CO flew on most of the squadron's raids; he didn't pick his targets, looking for the easier ones. He knew everyone on his squadron by first name, talked with them, drank with them, played games with them. He had a rapport with the groundcrew that grew out of genuine respect on both sides. He encouraged you to speak up; to forget rank. He gave his non-commissioned aircrew the same attention and consideration he gave his commissioned officers and on every conceivable occasion got the entire squadron together for an all-ranks bash. He commanded by example, by leading, by flying the hardest, and not through orders, regulations, and stupid demands. Such commanders were a special breed and the RCAF had very few.

Immediately above the squadron commander was the station commander, the CO of the base. He held the rank of Group Captain. The two squadron commanders, who held Wing Commander rank, reported directly to him. We felt sorry for the station CO's. They had joined the RCAF in the 1920's and 1930's and held permanent commissions. An officer appointed during the war held only temporary rank. When the RCAF expanded – exploded is a better word – from 4,000 to 225,000 men and women, these permanent officers received rapid, overnight promotion. They took command of the hundreds of new training bases opened in Canada and eventually overseas. Their ages ranged from thirty-five to fifty-five. Many were too young for the first war and too old to fly in the second. Few had flown anything larger than training aircraft and had little idea of four-engined bombers or operational flying. They sat behind a desk in their station headquarters, which suited most of them fine. Some did try to learn and flew occasionally as observers with a squadron CO, but their lack of operational experience and the age difference made them unable to communicate with young aircrew. Few of them understood, or seemed to care about, the strains and fears suffered by the crews. Unless you were an officer you never had direct contact with them. You never shared a drink or socialized. They remained locked in their offices or mess, removed from the realities of the aircrews.

It was these men who dealt so fanatically with the LMF cases. Their conduct, of course, was clearly visible to the crews, who could not understand them and who, with the arrogance of youth, disparaged anyone who hadn't flown a tour of ops. The same men were, alas, not hesitant about claiming medals, a subject that is still a sore point with many aged veterans. Medals, gongs as they were called, came from recommendations submitted by the squadron CO and the station commander to Group Headquarters. Naturally, their names headed the lists. When they couldn't justify a gallantry medal, they settled for an Order of the British Empire, the OBE. This became known to the crews as the "Other Bastards' Efforts." Over 300 were handed out in the RCAF. There were some exceptions, men who despite the age gap flew as squadron commanders and won very legitimate decorations in brilliant fashion. But not very many.

Aircrew also had gong hunters – guys who would do just about anything to win a medal and get a ribbon to wear on their tunic. Some went to great length to embellish their daring feats, often with complete disregard of the facts. Medals were awarded in priority fashion. The pilot first, followed by the navigator and then the bomb aimer; but the gunners, if they had shot down fighters, often superseded all crew members. It was rare for a wireless operator to get gonged and even rarer for a flight engineer. If you saw either wearing a ribbon you knew immediately he had done something really outstanding. Success was the criterion for gallantry awards and it was measured in interesting fashion. If a crew had wandered, lost, off track, and had been badly damaged by fighters or flak but had still managed to get home, the captain would often get an immediate award for bravery. Most often his crew would get nothing. The fact that he had been shot up in the first place through incompetency was never mentioned. He had been successful in getting home on less than four engines. If some of the crew had been killed or wounded, all the better, it made the recommendation for the medal read well. Crews who completed thirty trips without getting shot up or crashing in fog or getting hammered by fighters or ditching in the sea, were often overlooked. It was a terribly unfair situation, made worse by the wartime publicity that surrounded the granting of a medal.

The squadron commander, of course, always got a Distinguished Flying Cross, just for being CO. Not that some of them didn't deserve it, but it was a ritual. When the DFC became, in their opinion, too common, they opted for the next higher decoration and collected a Distinguished Service Order. After all, there were 4,000 DFC's awarded in the RCAF and one should have something more exclusive. Actually, they should have tried to get the Distinguished Flying Medal. Only 500, it is interesting to note, were awarded. But as officers they were ineligible for the DFM, which was the preserve of non-commissioned officers; those lowly sergeant aircrew types.

The highest award for bravery in the face of the enemy was the Victoria Cross. It was usually awarded posthumously, indeed the RAF seemed to prefer it that way. Many RAF commanders were quoted as saying, "There will be no live VC winners in my command." The RCAF had two of its members so honoured, both posthumously: one, a pilot in coastal command and one, an air gunner in No. 6 Group. Two Canadians flying in the RAF won VC's and these were also both posthumous awards.

The RAF awarded several VC's in Bomber Command. Three of the recipients lived to be presented to the King, who duly gonged them. But these justly deserved and incredible awards were frowned upon by the very senior commanders who, through a combination of jealousy and stupidity, thought any VC winner should be a dead man.

While many of the gallantry awards were richly deserved, the fact was that very many, who also deserved to be honoured, were ignored. To complete the irony each surviving winner today receives a cheque from the federal government. A regulation passed by Parliament in 1972 authorizes the payment of $50 a year to any holder of a gallantry medal. Our parliamentarians, bless their pointed little heads, decreed that this magnificent sum should be paid in twelve monthly instalments. Each qualified medal holder receives four cheques of $4.16, and eight cheques of $4.17, all tax free. However, the veteran can only collect for one medal. If he has others, too bad. Only one to a customer and God Save The Queen.

The government cheque is stamped "Gallantry Award." It must be confusing to those young female bank tellers who encounter them each month. The word gallantry alone is confusing, since it has been out of style in Canada for years. But in addition, I am sure they must wonder how much gallantry was expended for $4.16.

Those Magnificent Men

The magnificent contributions to Allied victory by the RCAF bomber force lie buried in dusty files and in the dimming memories of those who survived. Canadians as a whole, know little of the men developed by that tremendous force. It was nothing short of sensational that Canada could develop flyers of their magnitude in so short a time.

Men like Johnnie Fauquier. Men like Nellie Timmerman, Cam Mussels, Howie Morrison, Reggie Lane, Joe McCarthy, Hal Miles, Tiny Ferris, Bill Newson, Bill Swetman, Henry Carscallen, to name only a few. They were cast in the same mould as the RAF's Cheshire, Gibson, Martin, and Tait. They have never been acclaimed by their countrymen, which is a pity because they could teach the youth of Canada something of the spirit of those Canadians who, when thrust into danger, replied with unexcelled courage. Many stayed on in the peacetime air force and had exemplary careers, but some, like Johnnie Fauquier, shed their uniforms as quickly as they had first put them on.

To cite Johnnie Fauquier's record is almost to bore with its long list of accomplishments. Three tours of bombing operations, twice commanding the RCAF's only Pathfinder squadron. A request from Harris to lead what Harris considered to be his best squadron, No. 617, "Dam Buster" squadron – an accolade Harris had never conferred on any but his beloved RAF men. Fauquier led it to further glory, and he dropped a rank from Air Commodore to Group Captain to do it. Harris called those who kept going back on operations, the old lags. Fauquier was indeed an old lag. He had already completed two tours of operations and could, with his Air Commodore rank, have rested easily at a desk in No. 6

Group Headquarters, counting his medals. But Fauquier would have dropped back to Pilot Officer to get back into action, and he jumped at the chance to lead No. 617 squadron.

He was following in some big footsteps. The RAF's unexcelled Leonard Cheshire, VC, had to be forced by Harris to stop flying after 100 bombing raids. An unbelievable leader, he knew every man and woman on his squadron by their first names. Cheshire flew on all the tough raids and was literally worshipped by his men. They were, as they would proudly tell you, Cheshire Cats. It was Cheshire who single-handedly pushed for low level marking of targets, and finally overcame the opposition of Harris and his group commanders by his brilliant flying and marking. He marked the targets for the rest of us; first flying a Halifax, then a Lancaster, then a Mosquito, and finally a Mustang fighter. He came in over the roof tops, into the hell of every gun, and dropped his target indicators exactly on the aiming point. Circling at 200 feet he would continue to re-mark the target when the bombs from the main stream of bombers blew out the markers. In later operations he directed the main stream by radio, telling them to hold up while he re-marked, or telling them to press on, monitoring the entire attack from start to finish. He was built without nerves and we all knew it and marvelled. No. 617 squadron would have followed him through a brick wall. It is amazing that he received only one Victoria Cross. But, as already mentioned, the RAF had long held to the premise that any VC holder should be a dead one and it seemed to annoy some of them that Cheshire was still alive.

Guy Gibson had led No. 617 squadron on the famous Dam Buster raid that destroyed the dams north of the Ruhr Valley, and he too had won the Victoria Cross. Willie Tait, another 617 commander, had somehow escaped winning the VC but won four Distinguished Service Orders, a record for any service. They were worn immediately in front of his two DFC's.

The act of appointing a Canadian to lead this most famous of all heavy bomber squadrons was felt in some RAF quarters to be heresy, and Fauquier was tested hard when he assumed command. Aircrew with two tours of ops abounded on the squadron and the cynical attitude exhibited towards Fauquier's appointment was the first thing he had to defeat. He accomplished this with the same ease with which he led every raid. It was then late in 1944, and many of the aircrew had begun to relax and to rest on their oars, convinced the war was won and the rest just a formality. They had won the right to relax but Fauquier was a driver, a perfectionist who wanted to see the squadron maintain its efficiency to the very last day, and he drove them hard.

Barnes Wallis had now perfected his Grand Slam bomb. The enormous 22,000 pound bomb was the offspring of his 10,000 pound Tall Boy which had given great success against the V-1 sites and other specially hardened targets. No. 617 was the first squadron to drop this monster that could cut through thirty feet of reinforced concrete and explode deep beneath submarine pens. Designed to create an earthquake effect it was not necessary to score a direct hit; instead, the bomb was aimed immediately alongside viaducts and bridges. After it plunged into the ground for 100 feet, the tremendous underground explosion created a tunnel which collapsed the bridge into it.

Fauquier led 617 squadron on mission after mission throughout the spring of 1945. Railway lines, bridges, viaducts, tunnels, submarine pens, and other special targets received death blows. He went deep into the Baltic to find and sink the pocket battleship *Lutzow*, the second battleship sunk by the squadron. Finally, he ran out of targets, as the war dragged to a close.

Eager to see for himself the results of his special bombs, Barnes Wallis asked Harris for permission to go to the Continent to study their effect. Harris agreed, and instructed Fauquier to go along. Fauquier flew into Germany and landed near Hamburg, which although in German hands, was supposed to surrender that day. Nobody, it seems, had told the Germans. Unknowingly, Fauquier jeeped into the city to look at the massive submarine pens he had last seen from his bombing runs. While looking around the blasted ruins he and his party were surprised to find some 200 German sailors still working there. They immediately offered him their formal surrender and invited him to lunch. So another first for Fauquier; the only RCAF commander to accept a formal surrender from the enemy.

Johnnie Fauquier was old compared to the average aircrew. When he arrived in England in June 1941 he was thirty-two years old. A bush pilot before the war, he had already logged hundreds of flying hours. He was immediately pressed into flying instruction duties, a job he found depressing. He spent a frustrating year fighting to get posted overseas. When he did he led the first Canadian bomber squadron into action against Germany and continued to lead this squadron, No. 405, until forced into taking a rest from ops. He led the famous attack on Peenemunde, the secret German research base in the Baltic, where work on the V-1 and V-2 rockets was of crucial importance to the Germans. It was on this raid in August 1943 that he acted as one of the first Master Bombers, circling the target at very low level while directing the main bomber stream by radio. He not only led the 600 bombers, some sixty of them RCAF bombers, but stayed over the target for thirty minutes. The Germans managed to shoot down forty of his raiding force, but the attack was a success and set back production of the deadly V weapons for nearly a year.

A big man, Fauquier was brusque. He never said much, but his forceful manner and decisiveness eliminated the need for chatter. While his crews didn't love him in the manner of a Cheshire, they had enormous respect for his talents and courage. He led them by leading, by flying the hardest. He didn't think leading a squadron was a personality contest, but used his skill and courage to gain the necessary respect from his crews. His example in the air was a challenge to each and every one of them. Fauquier won the Distinguished Service Order three times, a feat no other Canadian accomplished in the war.

In one respect Fauquier was fortunate. He got the chance to lead special squadrons on special assignments, and thus to exhibit the natural talents he possessed in abundance. Conversely, he would not have been given the chance had he not sought out the leadership position. While there were other Canadians who got the chance to display their skills, the RCAF had insufficient numbers of squadrons to demand the right to plan their own air strikes. So for the most part the RCAF contented itself with bomber stream operations. Despite that fact, the RCAF produced some splendid squadron commanders and flight commanders.

The Wings Of A Dove

All of the heroes of the RCAF didn't wear Wings or fly aircraft. For every aircrew member singled out for special recognition there were thousands who went quietly about on more pedestrian, but essential tasks.

Royal Canadian Air Force Padres had one of the most difficult jobs, and one not fully appreciated or ever officially recognized. The range of their duties and responsibilities seemed to encompass the entire spectrum of air force life. It was they who stood in the rain and cold to comfort the crews before takeoff; they who were always there to greet them on return; they who gathered up the personal effects of those who never came back; they who wrote the heartfelt letters to the bereaved parents; they who visited the sick and wounded in hospital; they who buried the aircrew; they who interceded against wrathful commanders; they who gave fatherly counsel in tangled love affairs. Above all, it was the Padres who understood and helped carry the awesome fears of the young airmen.

One of the great things about those chosen by the Church to serve in the forces was their lack of secular rigidity. Different faiths never seemed to matter to them. Airmen brought up in one faith had little difficulty discussing personal problems with a Padre of another faith. This was particularly evident with the Jewish airmen. The RCAF did not have Rabbis. Jews, therefore, had recourse only to Protestant and Catholic chaplains, and yet very close relationships developed among many of them due to the calibre of the Padres.

The RCAF was blessed with many outstanding men of the cloth. Men who were fully in tune with the high spirits and reckless behaviour of the airmen who referred to them as "sky pilots." Everyone had his favourite Padre and mine was Norman Gallagher, the youngest chaplain to serve overseas in the war. This young Catholic priest had many outstanding qualities and perhaps foremost was his razor sharp wit. Combined with his humanness, intelligence, and warmth, it later made him a legend in the peacetime air force.

One of the duties our service Padres inherited during the war was the censorship of airmen's letters home. Any available extra hands considered officer status were also pressed into this distasteful work, including those of itinerant war correspondents who were covering the war for Canadian newspapers. Greg Clark, the diminutive imp who, with artist Jimmie Frise, had made the Toronto *Star Weekly* a household word with their brilliant feature stories, was one of those censors. Clark had won the Military Cross in the trenches of World War One and now, while covering this war as a correspondent, was to lose a son in the bitter ground fighting in Europe.

On his censoring duties Clark was paired with Father Gallagher, whose sense of humour equalled his, and the two became lifelong friends. To encounter them at the bar was to assure yourself of a great evening. Clark had been raised a Protestant and he loved to tease the young priest who came from Gravelbourg, Saskatchewan. At the same time he looked out for him in a parental way.

One day near the end of June, Clark started a conversation with Gallagher as they sat at a table covered in outgoing mail, snipping away with scissors at letters that supposedly contained military secrets. "You know of course, Norman, that I'm a staunch and loyal Orangeman, and the twelfth of July is just around the corner."

"Yes, I realize that," a puzzled Father replied.

"Well, I just want you to know that on the twelfth I won't be able to speak to you. I couldn't possibly have anything to do with a Catholic on the glorious twelfth."

Stunned at Clark's unexpected show of religious fervour, Gallagher said he didn't understand why the twelfth of July should intervene in their friendship. Clark went into a long explanation of his family's proud Protestant heritage. Of the glories of the Orangemen's Parade in Toronto, each twelfth of July. Of the magnificent sight of King Billy on his white horse, leading the thousands of orange-sashed marchers down Yonge Street. Of how his mother had started taking him to the parade as a small boy and how proud she was of everything Orange and Protestant and how disdainful of Catholics.

"It would be a terrible dishonour to my family, especially my mother. She would never understand that I had actually spoken with a priest on the twelfth of July. No, I can't possibly speak to you that day. I do hope you understand."

Bewildered, Gallagher accepted the situation.

As the days passed, Clark kept reminding Gallagher of the great day coming, dropping, almost as afterthoughts, small hints about the twelfth. "I suppose the airmen won't be allowed to parade. We could never find a white horse for one thing. Oh, well, it's enough just to remember all the glories of past parades."

Gallagher, who was busy with his work, failed to notice that five days prior to the twelfth Clark dropped the subject, without another mention.

On the morning of the twelfth, Gallagher had started censoring letters before Clark reported for duty. The first letter he opened was written by a corporal to his girlfriend in Canada. To his horror and astonishment Gallagher found that the letter was filled with the most bigoted religious beliefs. The corporal cursed priest-ridden England, the Pope, the Catholic Church, and blamed the entire war on the Catholics. The reason the corporal was stuck in the mud of England starving to death was because the Catholics were running the war. The letter went on and on in a similar vein. Completely upset and absorbed, Gallagher didn't notice Clark silently arrive and begin work. As he sat, head in hand, studying the letter, he finally looked up to find Clark sitting across the table busy at a pile of work. He immediately began relating the monstrous letter, that he, a priest, had to censor for military secrets, but which was full of the most outrageous nonsense.

"I can't possibly let this letter go through. Greg, you have no idea what I have just read."

Clark worked on in silence.

Unaware that he was talking to himself, Gallagher continued to justify his position. "I fully realize we are only to censor items that give military information, but really, Greg, there are moral grounds. This corporal's girlfriend will believe every word, and she'll spread this letter all over Canada. People will believe this nonsense."

Clark remained silent.

"Look Greg, what do you think I should do?"

Silence.

"I can't just ignore it, I have – " Gallagher started when he suddenly realized Clark had not spoken, had not even said good morning. Staring across at Clark he wondered why Greg wasn't speaking and then it hit him, it was the twelfth of July. Clark had said he wouldn't speak to him on that day. Panic stricken he began to plead with Clark.

"I know it's the twelfth, Greg, and you said you couldn't speak to me today, but you just have to help me with this awful letter. I can't pass it and I have no legal right to censor it. Please Greg, tell me what I should do."

Clark ignored his pleas and maintained his silence, dutifully snipping away at a letter.

"Please Greg, as a personal favour to me. Give me your advice. I promise not to bother you for the rest of the day."

Finally, with a great show of irritation Clark looked up, slowly and deliberately. "Norman, you have only one choice."

"What's that?" the young priest asked eagerly.

"Sign the letter," said Clark, "but sign it as a Roman Catholic priest. The girl will realize that you, a Catholic, have read the letter and have passed it without comment. This will prove to her and her friends that you fully agree with the principle of religious freedom and that you stand above petty cant."

Gallagher sat thinking for a long moment and then, convinced of Clark's logic, dutifully signed his name and title. He had barely finished the signature when Clark leaned over the table and whipped the letter from under his pen.

"Now," yelled a triumphant Clark, "off to Rome with this and we'll see what the Pope has to say about one of his priests agreeing with such blasphemy!"

It was only one of a large number of carefully worked out practical jokes that Greg Clark played on his unsuspecting friends. He had plotted this one for three long weeks, carefully arranging that the letter he had written would be the first that Gallagher opened on the morning of the twelfth of July.

When the invasion of Europe finally happened in 1944, the tactical air forces were able to establish airfields in France and Belgium. Gallagher was attached to them. So was John Clare, a squadron leader who had transferred to war correspondent duties. Clare, who was later to become managing editor of *Maclean's* magazine and who has always appreciated a good story, told me this one about Gallagher.

Gallagher, Clare, and a bunch of war correspondents were on leave in Brussels and were knocking a few back in a popular bistro that was filled with Allied soldiers. A group of American Army nurses just back from the horrors of a front line casualty hospital were also doing their best to forget the war. All were whooping it up in great style and Gallagher was enjoying the boisterous celebrating when suddenly the nurses decided to join the Canadian journalists.

One robust nurse was in great form and was leading the singing. She headed straight for Gallagher and throwing her arms around his neck, landed on his lap. It didn't phase Gallagher for a second and he began laughing and joking with the nurse. Clare, however, decided he should at least enlighten the nurse. "I think you should know, lieutenant," said Clare, tapping her on the shoulder, "that you are sitting on the lap of a Catholic priest."

With a great smile on his face, Gallagher immediately turned and said, "It's okay, John, I think I can handle this."

Norman Gallagher remained in the RCAF after the war, serving at various command headquarters in Canada and in the RCAF's NATO Air Division. In an unprecedented move in 1962 he was made a Bishop. This spectacular appointment, while richly deserved, caused some consternation at senior levels in the air force. It revolved around the fact that Gallagher was a Wing Commander which meant he had been elevated over a Group Captain and an Air Commodore. While still technically a Wing Commander he now carried a rank that outstripped anything military, and some senior officers found this hard to accept, especially since they had not been consulted about the appointment. Official eyebrows were raised. It was, however, a sensationally popular move with the airmen and junior officers. They arrived in Ottawa from all over Canada to attend and celebrate his confirmation to Bishop.

When Gallagher returned to France, where we were both stationed, I asked him about his first visit to Air Force Headquarters as a Bishop. He said with a great twinkle in his eye that he had been amused by the way very senior officers had jumped to their feet when he entered their offices. "I hope God will forgive me," he said, "for the thoughts that went through my mind."

Gallagher was an avid golfer and one time when we were stationed at St. Hubert, Quebec, we were invited to play the Montreal Country Club course by Don Long, a mutual friend and member of the club executive. The round progressed nicely until Gallagher sliced a drive and it went sailing out of bounds and through the window of a nearby house. Dismayed, the three of us trudged towards the house and towards the owner, standing on his back lawn, ball in hand. I could see Gallagher gathering his thoughts as we walked up to the man.

"I'm Father Gallagher," he began, only to be interrupted by an obviously Jewish voice. "Sorry, Father, but it's still $20 to you." He had been the third one that summer to break that same window and the owner had the replacement cost down pat.

I was able to lend him some clerical assistance one day that he never forgot. I had been sent as a replacement CO to a Mid-Canada Radar Line base in northern Quebec. Gallagher called me from Defence Headquarters at St. Hubert to tell me he was planning a visit to the base as part of the Chief of Staff's inspection party. I asked him if there was anything special I could do for him and he said no, he just wanted me to know he was coming. "I will be holding some masses on Sunday morning. It's not a big deal, only a handful ever turn out, but I'll need the use of the small warehouse."

The radar bases didn't have Chapels or permanent Padres and it was left to Gallagher and his fellow clergymen to hold religious services as best they could when they visited. Hanging up the phone, I called in the head of the civilian workers, who worked under contract for the Bell Telephone Company. The RCAF had only a handful of service people on those Mid-Canada Line bases but there were about 150 civilians employed. I suggested to the civilian boss that it would be nice if we had a maximum turnout on Sunday. "All Catholics, fallen or otherwise, shall be present for mass on Sunday, and all hands relieved of their duties, wherever possible, to ensure a full house."

When he arrived on the Saturday, Gallagher made his preparations to use the small warehouse for his church services. We helped him assemble the tables and chairs he would need. Since he carried a portable altar with him, he needed only some white tablecloths and odds and ends. He seemed quite pleased with the arrangements.

On Sunday, I was standing at the bar enjoying a pre-lunch beer when he confronted me.

"What," demanded an irate Gallagher, "did you do?"

"What are you talking about? Didn't anyone show up for mass?"

"You know very well they did. The church was packed. I never expected that crowd and hadn't prepared for them. I ran out of wafers and half of the men didn't have seats. Since I've never had more than a dozen attend a service here, you must be responsible."

"Nonsense. You're forgetting that this base is in Quebec and most of the guys are Catholics. You should have thought of that and planned accordingly." But he continued his harangue until I said, "Buy me a drink from the collection. It must have been a good one." This finally brought a smile to his face and got me off the hook.

I often wondered why Norman Gallagher stayed in the air force, and just what satisfaction he got from such service. I found out one day when I was visiting his office. A young leading aircraftsman came in. He was French Canadian and had difficulty with formal English.

"Father Gallacker," he said, "do you remember me?"

Gallagher smiled at the mispronunciation of his name and said, "I certainly do. Come in, Pierre, and sit down."

"No, Father, I have not time today. I just want for to say, you save my marriage. I have to catch a hairplane. Goodbye, Father."

When he left I asked Gallagher what the airman had meant. "Oh, he was having trouble with his marriage. His new bride couldn't understand the ways of the service and I helped them talk things out. We get lots of that. It's one of the great satisfactions. Makes the job worthwhile at times."

There were countless thousands of others that this jewel of a man helped. All with consummate ease and grace. He was also front and centre in the mess, and a party was never complete without him. The Friday night bash was called, TGIF, Thank God It's Friday. The RCAF used this term long before it was a popular phrase on civvy street. In those days, in Canada, Fridays were meatless days for Catholics. The mess had therefore to prepare fish as well as hamburgers to serve as snacks at those beer fests.

One Friday night, I caught Gallagher loading a huge hamburger onto a bun. "Ah, ah," I cautioned, "it's Friday."

He didn't hesitate, but took a thick slice of onion and laid it on the meat. "I hate onions," he said, "this will serve as penance."

That same night a farewell party had been arranged for a very popular officer who was retiring from the RCAF after a long and distinguished career. Like so many others named Harris, he was called Bomber. He had been a Wing Commander in 1941 and now years later was retiring as a Squadron Leader. He made this the theme of his farewell address.

"I'm sure that many of you are wondering how it is that a man could be a Wing Commander in 1941 and now, so many years later, be retiring a rank lower, as a Squadron Leader. Well we have only to turn to the Bible for the answer. As the Lord said in Acts 26:14, 'It is hard for thee to kick against the pricks.' "

As the crowd roared with laughter, Gallagher hurried out of the room in search of the mess Bible. We gathered around and sure enough there it was, the exact quotation. I think Gallagher secretly got more satisfaction from that episode than the rest of us. His military career was spent interceding on behalf of people who suffered under the pompous authority of mindless commanders.

Norman Gallagher retired from the RCAF in 1963 to take up full time duties as Auxiliary Bishop to the Armed Forces and finally as Bishop of Thunder Bay, Ontario. Here he contracted Parkinson's disease and spent the remaining years of his life in pain and poor health. But his spirit never diminished and he continued to lead his flock until the end came in 1975. Not many of his friends knew how sick he was, for his letters continued to sparkle and his humorous comments on the Canadian scene were as sharp as ever. There are countless thousands who will never forget Norman Gallagher.

Raid!

The American Eighth Air Force, which had begun bomber operations at the beginning of 1943 with a handful of B-17 bombers,
mushroomed as the year unfolded. They began by bombing the
easily reached coastal ports of Europe, having neither the numbers
of bombers nor the fighter escorts required for daylight raids of
deeper penetration. They were committed to the belief that accurate bombing could only be achieved in daylight, when you
could see the target. Dropping bombs at night or through cloud
was to them a futile and expensive waste. They approached the
problem in typical American fashion: overwhelm the defences and
shoot your way to and from the target. They knew the RAF had
abandoned daylight bombing because of their great losses to the
German fighters and so they planned accordingly. Each bomber
bristled with .5 inch machine guns, and the aircraft, while unable
to carry the bomb loads of the British bombers, could climb to
30,000 feet.

But it wasn't enough. They got chewed up by the swarming ME
109's and FW 190's and began to seriously doubt that daylight
bombing was possible. Fighter escorts were tried. At first, Spitfires
were used as protection, but the short ranged Spits could take
them only a short distance into enemy territory, and then they
were on their own and suffered heavy losses. If they were to reach
the Ruhr Valley and beyond they must develop a long range fighter
escort. Work began immediately in that direction. First the P-38
Lightnings flew as escorts, then P-47 Thunderbolts, and finally,
the key to success, the P-51 Mustang that was able to fly to Berlin
and back. But it took over a year to reach that position. In March
1943 the Americans could only muster 100 Fortresses for a raid. In

May it had grown to 300, by November 500, and in December they had 600 operational bombers. America had turned on the production tap and was building several four-engined bombers every hour and a merchant ship every four days. A staggering total of weapons was flooding into Britain, Africa, Burma, and the south Pacific.

Now the Allies could offer Germany round the clock bombing. Hardly had we landed from a night raid when the Eighth Air Force was taking off to stoke the fires and start new ones, driving the survivors underground once more. Shuttle bombing was tried. Using Russian and North African aerodromes, the bombers flew on after dropping their bombs, to regroup at foreign airfields and ready for the return raid which brought them back to base. This meant the Germans had to strengthen every area, every approach to Germany, as the aerial seige began. The German air defence network was now stretched from Norway to Italy, through all the occupied countries of Europe: a tremendous system of fighter bases, flak batteries, radar stations, searchlight batteries, and civil defence workers numbering in the millions.

As 1943 drew to a close and the Battle of Berlin continued it was announced that a total of 136,000 tons of bombs had been dropped on the enemy. Dreadful as that total was, it paled in comparison to what would happen in 1944. In the first two months of the new year, despite the many cancellations due to weather, the bombers were able to drop 36,000 tons, and in March, 20,000 tons.

The Battle of Berlin had opened in November 1943, when 400 bombers struck the city. Harris had decided to withdraw the older Stirling, Wellington, and Halifax aircraft and to rely mainly on the Lancaster. The Lancaster force was steadily increased so that by February 1944, 1,000 Lancasters were sent to Berlin to drop 2,500 tons of bombs in a single night.

As the Eighth Air Force built up its strength and the long range Mustang fighters were able to provide fighter protection, they too joined in the Berlin raids. In March 1944 they mustered 670 Fortresses and Liberators and, protected every mile of the way, dropped 1,600 tons of bombs on Berlin in a single raid. More to the point, they destroyed twice as many German aircraft as they lost. A new strategy had evolved; seek out the German fighters and destroy them in the air. Attack, not only with bombs but with the fighter escort, eagerly seeking encounters with the German

180

fighters. From this point forward the Americans were invincible, and began to range over Germany seeking the elusive oil refineries and aircraft factories.

Now the Allies were not only blasting the cities into rubble but blasting the Germans from the air and blasting the aircraft factories and synthetic oil refineries. The tide had turned and was irreversible.

Germany, in 1944, was pushed back behind her own borders for the first time in four years of war. The Allied armies invaded France and began to gobble up the German fighter bases, V-1 rocket sites, submarine pens, and coastal positions. Harris was able to get his OBOE blind bombing system installed on the Continent, greatly increasing its range and accuracy for pinpoint bombing. The American and British forces put their fighter bases in France and Belgium, and as the armies pushed towards the east, the Russians pushed west, and it became only a matter of time before total surrender.

But the German air force, the Luftwaffe, didn't seem to understand. They continued to attack the bombers, and bigger and bigger aerial battles were fought as air space diminished and attacks became more brutal. Thousands of crashed aircraft littered the routes across Germany. Bomber Command contributed over 7,000, more than 1,000 of them Canadian bombers. The Americans lost slightly more, and the Germans over 20,000.

But there were many bloody nights for Bomber Harris' bombers before the D-Day landings and capture of the occupied territories would permit him to return to daylight bombing. He was ordered, and then finally forced, to bomb tactical targets that would help the armies' imminent invasion. Until he could no longer resist the pressure, he continued his single-minded attack on the big cities of Germany, determined to bring the war to an end by bombing alone. His fixation on this single course led to the bloodiest night and the greatest slaughter we faced in that miserable winter.

On the night of March 30, 1944, Harris launched 800 bombers against Nuremberg. Of the 800 bombers, only some 750 actually attacked. Of these 97 were shot down. Twelve more were fatally damaged, and scores were ripped by flak and cannon shells, their crew members killed or wounded. The loss rate was 12 per cent. It was my last raid of the war. It was the most terrifying of all.

Nuremberg lies deep in southwest Germany, some 100 miles north of Munich and almost as far as the Lancaster could reach with a full bomb load. Everything seemed normal the day of the raid. When we were awakened that morning with the fatal words, "You're on, tonight," it meant nothing extra. Four nights earlier we had gone to Essen in the Ruhr Valley and the total losses were only nine aircraft. It had been successful because we had surprised the defences who had anticipated another raid on Berlin.

On that fateful morning we began the customary checks of S Sugar, looked over our flight gear, and were finished long before lunch. Then it was wait. Wait it out, as usual, wondering where we might be headed that night. Briefing was scheduled for 1600 hours and when it finally arrived we learned we were going to Nuremberg, which really meant nothing to our crew, except it was going to be a long stooge.

Takeoff for Nuremberg would be at 2200 hours and so the long wait continued. We roamed the base. Tossed a football around with the groundcrew for a while. Visited the recreation centre for ping pong and finally flopped into the mess to watch the ground types knock back the beer. Waiting, waiting, it killed the normal exuberance of the crews, as each in his own way struggled with his fears. It was a listless bunch of kids who tried the English darts and dominoes, or faked interest in the card games. The last supper; bacon and eggs. Normally they tasted great and took your mind off flying, but they could turn bland and tasteless on some nights, as you checked your watch again and again, waiting for the time to dress.

Finally, the long day dragged to a close and it was time to put on the flying gear. The sudden mingling in the crew room brought some life to the squadron and the corny jokes and one liners got more than their deserved share of laughter.

"Does mother know you're flying tonight?" a voice would call out. Then in falsetto tones, "Remember son, fly low and slow."

"Anyone want to leave their girlfriend's phone number with me?"

"I got a new parachute today and they told me to bring it back if it didn't work." Old, tired jokes.

Then the long, dreary ride in the dark to the far side of the field, piled four deep in the shadowy confines of a van. Jammed in with all the flying gear and flight bags we bounced and jostled our way to the kites. Crews disentangled themselves as the WAAF driver cheerily called out the bomber's letter at each dispersal point. "All right, S Sugar, here you are, then."

We tumbled out to find the groundcrew standing around in the dark, still fussing over the bomber and putting the fire extinguisher and battery cart in position for starting the engines. With a half hour until takeoff time we sprawled on the ground, those who smoked taking a few final drags on cigarettes that would be their last for the next eight hours. The Padre pedalled up on his bicycle to mumble a few words of encouragement, mostly about the weather. We appreciated his thoughtfulness, but felt sorry for him since he had difficulty talking to us about the purpose of the flight. Now I noticed Eric bent over the tail wheel and I could hear the choking sounds as he vomited, which told me it was time to climb on board. He came back to the rest of us to say, "Okay, gang, time to climb aboard."

Steve, the bomb aimer, went first, as we clustered around the small rear door, waiting to climb the short ladder. We gave Steve, who weighed 225 pounds and was clad in a huge, leather flying suit, time to make his way to the nose of the aircraft. We heard him grunting in the dark guts of the bomber as he tried to scramble over the main spar. I was next in the pecking order, arranged so the guys with the farthest to travel went first in order to avoid confusion in the dark confines of the Lancaster.

Once inside, groping forward, the smells of oil and grease, gasoline and paint dope washed over me. All aircraft smell, and the smells are either reassuring or stomach heaving, depending on the person. Personally, I liked the smells. They gave me a sense of knowing where I was; that things were familiar. As Stan pulled the ladder in and slammed the door a feeling of finality descended and I felt committed.

Settling into the pilot's seat, I hooked up my intercom and oxygen hose and fastened my shoulder harness before beginning the starting-up checks. Finally, I leaned out of the cockpit window to the waiting groundcrew and said, "Ready for starting." They had already pulled the propellers through a few revolutions by hand to test for hydraulic locking. This often happened on the Hercules engines. If they didn't revolve easily you knew oil had seeped into the cylinders, and to start an engine in that condition meant breaking the crankshaft or connecting rods.

Switches on, fuel on, mixture rich, propellers fully fine, throttles cracked open a shade, brakes locked on. I signalled to the port-inner engine and with the groundcrew shining a torch on the prop, I pressed the starter button. The engine coughed into life, quit, coughed, and then settled into a roar. I brought the throttle up slowly, watching the rev counter settle on 800 revs. After all four engines had started the groundcrew pulled the electrical cord from the fuselage and stood by to pull the wheel chocks. Quickly, I ran the engines one at a time to full power, checking the magneto switches and looking for a mag drop, while Jock checked the engine instruments for pressure and temperature readings. The Lanc danced on its tail wheel as a fully revved engine blasted the grass flat behind the dispersal. I called the crew, in turn, on the intercom to ensure they had done their checks and everything was working.

Then a wave of the hand to the groundcrew and they pulled the heavy wooden wheel chocks from in front of the main wheels. Clear to taxi. The engines strained as I opened the four throttles and released the air brakes. I rolled forward a few feet and then applied full brake to check that they worked, the air blasting and hissing as I released the brakes. I turned onto the dispersal track that led to the end of the runway, following a long line of bobbing bombers hardly visible except for their navigation lights.

Around the long narrow track I went, juggling the throttles and brakes to round the curves. Thirty Lancasters, mixed together from the two squadrons, lined up on each side of the runway waiting for their turn to take off. When the aldis lamp blinked towards me I moved forward and turned into wind on the runway. I watched the Lanc in front of me slowly gather speed as it thundered down the runway, its prop wash rolling back and rocking S Sugar.

A final, swift cockpit check and a call to the crew. I set the directional gyro to the compass heading and checked again that the pitot head was on and the bomb doors closed. Okay, twenty degrees of flap, all set. I opened the four throttles slowly, but firmly, until the Lanc was straining against the brakes, the engines screaming as I waited for the green light that would be flashed from the control van to my left.

Okay to go. I released the brakes and firmly moved the four

throttles forward, leading with the two on one side to counter the torque. Full rudder to check the swing. Slowly the swollen Lanc lurched forward as my eyes darted back and forth from the rev counters to the directional indicator to the runway lights. Stick forward to get the tail up as quickly as possible and provide better steering. Now, as the tail rose, I could open all four engines, and I pushed the throttles through the gate for maximum power and centred the rudder pedals.

Check the heading and airspeed, watch as the airspeed creeps past 90 then 100 and then 110. Ease back on the stick, using elevator trim to fly it off. No sudden yank that may jerk you up and stall the aircraft. Pray that an engine doesn't quit or you're a dead duck. Wheels up, throttles back to climbing power, revs back to 2,850 as we thundered into the dark, dragging over the trees for miles as I carefully milked up the flaps. A quick check that temperatures and pressures were all normal and I turned gingerly onto the first course and began the long climb that would take us to maximum height of 20,000 feet. I could feel the sweat under my leather helmet trickle down my neck, but the heat felt good after the clammy ground temperatures of the English March day.

Our track to Nuremberg lay across London, which wasn't the first time our astute planners had routed us that way. The Big Smoke could be as rough as some targets. The jittery army gunners always cut loose at you, despite the fact we were flying north to south and there were 800 of us. We could hardly be Germans to the most imaginative mind and yet they always pounded up the flak. But no one seemed to tell the army . . . or maybe they did. This time it was no different, but I was always startled and never ready for the flak bursts that rocked the Lancaster.

On most trips I really only got the adrenalin flowing when the bomb aimer said, "Enemy coast ahead, skipper." Flying over London was the exception. As usual I asked Eric to fire off the colours of the day as I weaved the Lanc around in the flak. As usual he put the cartridge in the Very pistol mounted in the roof of the aircraft and the colours of the day, which announced we were friends, arched into the sky. And as usual the flak continued. The army blazed away merrily until we had outrun their guns. Since we weren't over enemy territory our normal intercom silence was broken as everyone had something unpleasant to say about the "fucking army." "Those stupid bastards, wouldn't I like to drop this load right on them." "No wonder they never hit the Huns, they can't even hit us!"

The crew settled down as we continued the long climb towards France, waiting for the searchlights to come on along the coast. The coastal defences stretched the length of the Continent, and layer upon layer of searchlights and flak batteries guarded every foot. Only some twenty miles deep on the average they nevertheless were formidable, and I was glad to get through them. Once safely past, you faced only point defences mounted around each town and city and, of course, the roving bands of night fighters. The exception was the Ruhr Valley, where the defences surrounded the entire length and breadth of the German industrial heartland, making it a long continuous sea of lights and flak.

As we crossed the coast of France and flew on towards Nuremberg, I suddenly realized for the first time that it wasn't really dark. A full descending moon lay on the horizon to the south, playing on a very thin layer of cirrus cloud. Below, at 15,000 feet, a solid layer of stratus cloud stretched to the horizon. The cloud looked pristine and I could see our bombers starkly outlined by the white backdrop. We were flying in a well-lighted arena and were now high enough to produce beautiful vapour trails that streamed behind each bomber. I could see every rivet on the wings of S Sugar and it slowly dawned on me that, my God, we're flying in absolute daylight! I raised my seat, straining against the shoulder harness and rudder pedals to turn and look back the length of the aircraft. Ken was clearly visible in his mid-upper turret and I could see Stan swinging his rear turret back and forth, the moon glistening off the perspex. This was new and different. Never before had we been sent off in moonlight. Normally one never saw any part of the aircraft, except when silhouetted over the target. I could feel myself getting panicky, a strange fear creeping in despite the fact that we were not under attack. My fear grew as I swung my gaze around the sky. Bombers everywhere. I could count a dozen on the port side. My gawd, if the German fighters are up tonight, we've had it.

Eric was having trouble navigating and reported we seemed away ahead of schedule. The Gee was now being jammed by the Germans and he was unable to get a fix, but figured we were ahead of where we should be. "It's probably the winds," he reported.

We had been given wind speeds of sixty miles an hour, almost dead on our tail, but obviously they were much stronger. Our track lay south of the Ruhr and north of the Rhine Valley and already we could see the searchlights to the north of us. We had already reached the Ruhr. We were to learn days later that the Mosquito crews who regularly checked the winds aloft with their sophisticated navigation instruments, had radioed that the winds were 100 miles an hour at 20,000 feet. No one at headquarters had believed they could be that strong and so sixty miles an hour was used to plot the course and time the trip. Actually, they were 120 miles an hour and the entire bomber stream would reach the target well ahead of schedule, some even before the Pathfinders had found the target.

Real apprehension gripped me and I was startled at the way I was behaving. I warned the gunners to look sharp and keep the turrets swinging. As we moved south of Aachen, the German fighters swept in to attack. I watched horrified as a twin-engined fighter flew up the white vapour trails of the bombers on my left. Lancasters were rearing up in flames, exploding into fireballs as their bomb loads blew up and they plunged over and down. Others were being hit with cannon shells, fire racing along their wings as they began the long drop through the clouds below, parachutes filling the sky as the desperate crews tried to abandon the wrecks. Tracers were lacing and criss-crossing in the sky as the German cannons found the range. I could see the smaller machine gun tracers from the bombers flicking out of the turrets, the rear gunners continuing to fire as their stricken bombers fell out of control.

I had never before experienced the fear that was gripping me. It was totally irrational; our aircraft wasn't under attack despite the butchery going on all around us. I told myself to calm down, that this was no different from previous raids. But it was different. I could smell the danger. We, like all the others, were sitting ducks, silhouetted against the solid cloud layer below, lit by the diffused light of the moon, and leaving large, white vapour trails to mark our exact positions. We had never before been able to see the bomber stream over Germany.

Flying the Lancaster was now a totally automatic thing and I wanted to do more to protect it, to somehow become more involved with my destiny. I braced against the seat with my shoulders, straining against the seat harness to arch up and look in all directions. I searched the sky; everywhere I could see bombers, the fighters zipping in and around them, their tracers flashing.

"Stan, do you see that fighter at five o'clock low?"

"Yeah, I've got him," Stan answered immediately. Then quickly in surprise, "Is that you skipper?"

"Yes, it's me."

"Jesus, you mean you can see him, too?"

"I can see from here to Russia," I yelled, "and you guys better be alert. We're a sitting duck in this shooting gallery!"

My feet actually chattered on the rudder bars as my fear continued. God, will this trip never end? There was nothing to take my mind off the horrors of the night and I felt completely helpless. I continued to roll the Lanc back and forth, searching, searching. The fighter attacks continued as we swept along in the 120 mile an hour wind towards the target. Dim shapes suddenly erupted into balls of fire as bomber after bomber blew up, their explosions lighting the sky and then slowly fading as they disintegrated, the pieces falling to earth.

The crew were silent, frozen with fear, awaiting the attack we were sure would come. It never came. With the moon flooding the sky, we were being swept through the bloodiest night Bomber Command ever faced, without a scratch. No time to wonder why. Search, search the sky and search the sky again. Weave the Lanc, for God's sake, keep the Lanc rolling, diving, climbing. Pray.

Eric called me to say we were a half hour from the target. "Like hell we are," I replied. "I can see it from here!"

A white face appeared over my shoulder and a voice said, "Christ, what's going on?" It was Eric. He normally flew under a blackout curtain which pulled completely around his navigation table. This shielded his table light from prying eyes. He, like so many navigators, rarely emerged from behind his curtain. We could see flares going down and flak hosing up the searchlight beams as the first wave of bombers began ripping red blotches under the cloud layer. Eric and I were unsure if this was the right target and as we studied the situation another attack started due south. It looked much larger than the one immediately ahead.

"That must be Nuremberg farther south. These guys are bombing the wrong target," Eric said. I swung away to the right to miss the fire from whatever town this was and then turned south once more, sweat trickling down under my arms, my mouth dry. The moon finally slipped below the horizon and we were back in the familiar and welcome darkness.

It was another fifteen minutes before we knew for certain that the target now ahead of us was much larger than the first one. Fires had begun sweeping through Nuremberg and the fierce flak and rising smoke proclaimed a major target. Pushed by the fierce winds, our bomb run was the shortest I ever experienced. Hold it level, ignore the lights and flak, concentrate on straight and level flying. My brain told me this was the crucial point of the whole trip. Why fly through all this hell and quit at the last minute? Why not? a small voice whispered. Because if we don't bomb it tonight they'll send us back tomorrow night to do it all over again. But it would be so easy to turn away and let the bombs fall where they liked. Hell, they're all big cities, surely the bombs would hit something. Hold it steady. Eternity surely couldn't last this long.

Bomb doors open and vibrating against the airstream. It was only at this time you remembered the bloody doors were thirty-two feet long. Airspeed steady at 160 miles an hour. Hold it right at 20,000 feet. Keep your eyes on the flight instruments. Concentrate. Never mind the insanity outside the cockpit.

Feet vibrating on the rudder bars, I waited for Steve's directions. Hurry up you stupid bastard, have you fallen asleep? Steve was methodical, but he was accurate and hated to hurry. He had flown over three hours to perform his one important function and he never wanted it hurried.

"Left, left, skipper," he finally called.

I touched the left rudder.

"Left, left," he said again.

This time I jabbed hard at the bar. Sure enough.

"Right, skipper."

I flicked the right rudder.

"Steady . . . steadyyy. Hold it. Bombs gone."

"Bomb doors closed," I yelled, not waiting for his order as I snatched up the lever and swung away off the target. Then pushing the throttles up I continued the turn until I had settled on the course Eric had given me before the bomb run.

Now for the long haul home, dead into the wind that had pushed us so fast to the target. I could see two fires burning as we flew northwest. I never learned what the first target was, but suspected it must be Schweinfurt. I never really cared enough to find out. With those unexpected winds it was a miracle the Pathfinders had found even one. Not knowing the real windspeed we continued using sixty miles an hour to plot the westward course.

Our route lay across France. Ceaselessly the gunners swung their turrets, searching in the recommended search pattern – across, up, across, down, across – trying to cover each segment of the sky in sequence but suddenly reversing when their eyes thought they detected a shadow or something moving. Now and again a brilliant flare lit the sky as the German fighters dropped parachute flares to light the bomber stream. They hung for a long time, the dazzling white light visible for miles. If you were close to one it was possible to see every inch of your aircraft. Then there were the scarecrows, the huge balls of fire they dropped to simulate exploding aircraft and make the crews feel nervous. It made you acutely aware the sky didn't belong to Bomber Command and there were unfriendly people around.

Endlessly the hours dragged by as we plodded west. The roar of the four engines was a constant but reassuring noise that crept into your very bones as the aircraft vibrated and the instrument panel jiggled. The steady roar of the engines in the unpressurized bombers was as wearying as anything else about the raids and my head rang for hours after a flight, especially if I had a head cold.

Several more explosions erupted around us, some close enough to make me swerve the Lancaster quickly as the tracers pursued the bomber stream. Tracers flashing across the sky in front of your nose gave the impression they were meant for you. It was only when I desperately dove down and away that I found where they were headed, as a bomber burst into flames directly ahead.

Tracers. They were the only warning you got. If they missed you on the first burst, there was time to fling the bomber away and elude the radar operator in the German night fighter who couldn't adjust quickly enough. If they hit on that first burst they were usually successful in hitting an engine or rupturing the gas tanks. The German cannon fire was far more effective than the small calibre machine guns we carried and just a few shells could smash the fragile skin of the bombers. Except for those tracer shells we would never have known a fighter was there, and I would wonder why they used them. Stare and search the black sky as hard as you wished, it was usually impossible to spot the small fighters. Since we were defenceless from attacks beneath the aircraft, the Germans became adept at sneaking under and then pulling straight up to aim for the bomb bay. The ground radar that directed them by voice signals was excellent, and put them into position where they could take over visually for the attack. The twin-engined fighters had a radar operator on board, and once the ground radar had placed the fighter in the bomber stream, he took control and directed the pilot.

In an attempt to counter the threat, the RAF had developed a small radar set called Monica, which was monitored by the wireless operator. Its beam was directed to the rear of the bomber and was supposed to pick up the fighters as they approached. But in the bomber stream there was such a clutter of blips from our own machines that it was ineffective and, I thought, dangerous. Some rear gunners were nervous and when Monica made them think they were being attacked they fired on their own aircraft (following the old dictum, fire first and ask questions later). Monica did give the wireless operator something to do and kept his fingers out of his mouth, but that was about all. I objected to the constant chatter from the wireless operator to the gunners. This blocked the intercom for other uses and after one trial I never used Monica again.

We flew on towards the distant coast as I watched the clock approach 0400 hours. "Where in hell are we, Eric?" I called.

"Just a minute, skipper, I'm trying to get a fix on the Gee box."

Silence again. We flew steadily on, weaving our way west. Then, "Skipper, the Gee is jammed. I don't know where we are, but we must be getting close to the coast." For the first time ever, I noticed panic in Eric's voice.

"Okay, Eric." I tried to keep my voice calm and even. Flapping wasn't going to get us home. But a half hour later I called him again. "Any luck with the Gee box, Eric?"

"Not yet, the box is a mass of wavy green grass. But according to my dead reckoning plot we must be close to the sea."

"Keep trying," I replied. "Steve," I called the bomb aimer, "keep a sharp lookout for the coastline. The cloud bank often has breaks over the sea." Steve blipped his mike switch in reply. We stooged on westward with the compass reading 280 degrees.

Ten minutes later Eric called. You could hear the fear in his voice. "Skipper, I think we've overshot the coast and are headed out to sea."

I stiffened. My mind raced. Is that possible? To overshoot the coast on this heading would put us parallel with the south coast of England and headed into the north Atlantic. But if that's so then the Gee box should be free of the German jamming and should be working. But Eric says it's still jammed which means we are likely still over France somewhere. It was the only clue I could think of that seemed logical. Must be those bloody headwinds, God they must be ferocious.

As calmly as I could, I told Eric to relax. "I think we're okay Eric, we'll get a fix on the Gee soon. The winds are a lot stronger than we figured." Only partly convinced, my thoughts turned immediately to our fuel. We had been airborne for six and a half hours and only God knew how much farther we had to go. We still had to find England, and then it would take an hour to fly north to Yorkshire. Jock checked the gas and reported 600 gallons remaining.

"We're all reet, lad, plenty of petrol," Jock spoke up. This little bastard hasn't got a nervous bone in his body, I thought. Jock never got excited on a trip; at least if he did he kept it to himself. He rarely spoke throughout the entire flight. He kept himself busy with his engine instruments and gauges and recorded everything in his log in a precise, almost copperplate script.

We pressed on in the dark, seeing nothing and feeling terribly alone. Often you would get behind another bomber and be rocked by his slipstream, even though you couldn't see him. While annoying, it was also reassuring. Nothing like that happened tonight. The wind had obviously dispersed the stream over hundreds of miles. We were alone, with the cloud thickening. Cut off from all contact with the earth, unable to get a star shot for astro navigation, we were dependent upon the Gee to find our position. My mind continued to grapple with Eric's statement that we were headed out to sea. How, if the Gee box didn't begin working, would we ever know?

Another half hour went by before an excited Eric called to say the Gee was starting to work and he should have a fix in a minute. Then, "Okay skipper, we'll cross the coast in twenty minutes. Change course to 305 degrees."

"Roger, 305 degrees."

Eric, as usual, was right on. Soon flak began rocking the Lanc which announced we were over the coastal defences. It was almost a welcome relief from the dreaded uncertainty of the last hours. Now we were flying in solid, unbroken cloud, as we steered for England and home.

"Ray," I called the wireless operator, "see if you can raise base for a weather check." I didn't want to fly the length of England to find our base socked in by weather. We got the bad news almost immediately.

"Skipper, all bases in northern England are closed. They advise some might be open in the south."

"Isn't that bloody marvellous," I replied. "The planners sure had their finger in tonight. I wonder what genius planned this trip?"

"Butcher Harris, who else?" Steve said.

I began descending below 10,000 feet as soon as Eric called us over the English coast. Now at last we could get those suffocating oxygen masks off our faces. I called, "Oxygen off, you guys." I got the reply I always got.

"Okay to smoke, skipper?" It was Davidson in his mid-upper turret, of course.

"No. Wait until we get down. There could be German fighters around. Keep those bloody turrets moving." Since I didn't smoke I didn't understand why anyone needed a cigarette. Today, as a constant cigar smoker, I wonder they didn't lynch me. "Ray, get on the set and find a base that's open," I added.

Five minutes later he came on the intercom. "There's a base called Morton-In-Marsh still open, skipper, but they say to hurry. Their ceiling is down to 200 feet and it looks like it will clamp in."

"Eric, where in hell is this place?"

"Second, skipper." Eric was all business and his usual efficient self. A crackerjack navigator in whom I had tremendous faith. I continued to let down to safety height as we turned northwest and headed for Morton-In-Marsh. These wonderful English place names, I thought. Too bad it's not Little Snoring, exactly what we need at the moment.

I broke cloud at 200 feet directly over the base. Morton-In-Marsh was an Operational Training Base flying old Whitley and Wellington twin-engined bombers and hadn't the longer runways of the four-engined bomber bases. Throwing the Lanc into a left hand circuit I dropped the landing gear and pushed down twenty degrees of flap, checking my height to keep below the cloud and keep the base in sight.

Morton-In-Marsh had a glide path indicator, a luxury for a training base. Erected on a pole beside the runway it looked like a traffic signal, except the red light was on the bottom and the green on top, with the amber in the centre. The theory was simple. If you could see the red light you were too low; the amber told you to be careful you could be slipping into the red; and the green light meant your angle of approach was just right. But it was set for the Wellington's glide and flight angle and not the Lancaster's.

I believe to this day I was in the green on the entire approach, brief as it was. I tightened the left hand turn to keep the runway in sight. As I flew over the button of the runway it was immediately obvious that I was too high and too fast. But I wasn't going around again, even though the runway was 1,000 feet shorter than our home base.

I slammed the Lanc down, yelling at Jock to hold the throttles back as we began to float between the runway lights. On and on we floated, the end of the runway lights looming. "Get down, you black bastard," I muttered, and slammed the main wheels on the pavement. I pulled hard on the brake lever as the main wheels held, but released them as the nose began to dip down. I held the control stick hard back, then pulled the brake lever full on for the second time. But back flew the runway lights, and then we were off the end, bumping over the grass in total darkness. Stop, you miserable bitch! But we kept on bouncing over the rough ground. Then *bang, plop*. The main wheels bounced into a narrow ditch. Jock had cut the fuel and ignition switches as we had left the runway. Miraculously there was no damage. The props hadn't even touched the ground.

We were down. Too exhausted to move I slumped there in my seat. It was six o'clock in the morning. We had flown for seven and a half hours and still had another hour to fly to get back to base. We had been out of bed for twenty-two hours. The King, I thought, has really got his shilling's worth.

A crash truck eventually arrived and we all climbed slowly and silently into it for the ride to the operations centre for debriefing. But the officer in charge of night flying found us first. He came panting up as we unloaded from the crash truck.

"Were you in the green on the glide path?"

Bewildered by the question I said, "Yeah, I'm sure I was."

"I knew it. I knew it! The bloody thing is out of alignment. I've argued all night but they won't change it. This proves I'm right. Thanks." With that he trotted off.

Oh, to be in England.

Accidentally Army

The magic words, "You're screened," fell on my ears one afternoon, shortly after we had returned from Morton-In-Marsh. Our crew was throwing a football around on the grass in front of the flights. Squadron Leader Stewart yelled the words from the doorway. Stunned, I stopped and stared as at first the words failed to sink into my brain. Screened? No more ops? I've finished my tour! A bittersweet feeling overcame me and I found I couldn't reply. I looked around. Far off across the airfield I could see the Lancasters parked. No more raids. No more S Sugar. Screened. The familiar sights and sounds of squadron life would be no more. No more terrified flights in the dark. I knew I was pleased and yet a tug of regret nagged at me. How could I leave this place? This was where the war was fought. This is what I had come overseas to do. I would have to leave my crew. We would be split up.

"How do you know?" I finally yelled back at Stewie.

"A signal just came in from Group. It's official. You're screened."

It was mid-April 1944 before the parties ended and I said goodbye to my crew as we went our separate ways to training bases. This time we went as instructors. The signal which directed me said, "You are posted to RAF Station Honeybourne." There I found aircraft called Wellingtons and Martinets. I had flown Wellingtons during my training days but the single-engined Martinet was different. It was used primarily as a fighter trainer, and those pilots destined for Spitfires did some flying in them. They intrigued me, and I managed to get assigned to the fighter affiliation flight which used the Martinets to attack the Wellingtons. No crew to worry about and only one engine. Just myself alone in the sky. It was a great feeling after mothering a crew for so long, and the flying was far faster than in the Lancaster.

Part of the job was attacking the sprog Wellington crews undergoing training, making fake fighter attacks on them at night, coming up behind them and closing in until I turned on my landing light and illuminated the rear turret. Then the Wellington would go into a wild dive and begin corkscrewing around the dark sky. Never once did the rear gunner spot me before I shone the light on him, sometimes from as close as fifty yards directly behind. It brought back all those nights when I had thought no enemy fighter could ever shoot me down. God, how simple it was to get in behind those Wellingtons.

I had just finished attacking a Wellington one night and it had broken away to carry out a cross-country flight, when I noticed the sky was suddenly full of navigation lights. They were streaming south across our aerodrome by the hundreds. My gawd, what are all those aircraft doing? Unable to descend through them, I circled above as they streamed across the field at 1,000 feet. They were Dakotas and they were pulling gliders and the sky was full of them. It took nearly an hour for the parade to pass.

Upon landing I rushed into the operations centre to learn the reason for all those aircraft. No one knew. But we all guessed. D-Day had arrived. The sixth of June, 1944. We learned about it the next day and so did the world; the invasion of Europe was on. The war began to change dramatically from that moment.

One month after the invasion I was visiting London, frequenting the usual haunts when I fell ill with a very high fever. I staggered over to the RCAF Overseas Headquarters to find a doctor. After a long wait, one finally looked at me and said, "You have a temperature of 105 degrees. You'd better go into hospital." He arranged for an ambulance and I was driven north to Watford. Just about in a coma by the time I got to hospital, I didn't care whether I lived or died. The orderlies dumped me in a bed in a large ward and I didn't get my bearings for several days. It turned out that I had rheumatic fever.

When I finally felt like looking around at my new home I found I was one of twenty-five military types in a ground floor ward of a Canadian Army Hospital belonging to the RCAMC. Two of us were RCAF, the rest were army officers who had been wounded in France. The nurses were all Canadian girls, the first I had seen for more than two years. My recovery began from that moment.

In the bed next to me was a Flight Lieutenant from Philadelphia. Vince Schenk was a fighter pilot and one of the first Americans to join the RCAF. He had trained as a fighter pilot but had reached England too late for the Battle of Britain and in a period when the emphasis had switched to bomber operations. Vince and I became great friends as we swapped stories and played cards to wile away the long hours.

Vince had been asked if he would like to volunteer for flying duties aboard specially equipped ocean freighters. Since it sounded so bizarre he became interested. He asked why they would fly a fighter off a merchant ship. They told him the Germans were molesting the convoys with high flying Condor four-engined bombers that were sent out from France to spy on the ships and to direct U-boat attacks. The Admiralty had come up with the idea of putting a Hurricane fighter on some of the cargo ships to shoot down the Condors. The Hurricane was placed on a steam-driven catapult on deck and when a Condor appeared, the Hurricane was launched to the attack.

Intrigued with the idea, and with the thought he might get home to America for a visit, Vince had volunteered. He said it was the worst duty he had yet experienced. He had sat for days pounding through the seas on the pitching freighter, seasick and surrounded by sailors who thought him some kind of freak. The Hurricane fighter sat on its catapult and Vince sat on his bunk below decks, completely pissed off, waiting for a signal that a Condor was approaching.

When finally one did come, he climbed into the fighter and fired up the engine, while the crew prepared the launching apparatus. With a wave to the crew and securely fastened by his seat harness, he gave the thumbs up signal for launching. The powerful steam-driven engine erupted in a shower of steam and Vince was fired over the bows of the ship like a cannonball. The whiplash effect wasn't the major drawback to this ingenious system of fighter defence. Once airborne there was no way to land back on a freighter. Unlike an aircraft carrier, it had no flight deck; instead, it had a mass of funnels, winches, and booms. The pilot was instructed to bale out well ahead of the convoy and let the Hurricane crash into the sea. The pilot was then fished out as the ships approached him, bobbing in the freezing north Atlantic, held up by his Mae West lifejacket. If the convoy was under attack from U-boats it was reluctant to stop to rescue the pilot.

When Vince got airborne he found the Condor had turned back to its base and the threat was over. So he used the rest of his fuel doing aerobatics over the convoy and getting the most out of his brief trip. Finally he had rolled the Hurry over and baled out. He was fished out and spent the rest of the voyage as a passenger, since his only aircraft was now at the bottom of the ocean. When the ship returned to England Vince decided that his future lay elsewhere, and transferred back to a fighter squadron. Injured in a flying accident he was now recovering when I arrived to brighten his life.

The wounded army officers, some with desperate wounds, some with arms or legs missing, and many with horrible burns, made up the rest of the ward – except for a Padre who was being treated for syphilis. This was my first real experience with army types and they fascinated me over the next two months. It all started with the Padre. Once those army guys discovered his ailment their behaviour was nothing short of brutal. Their early morning taunts and wisecracks drove him crazy. For some strange reason they all came awake about four o'clock in the morning and, I suppose, surprised to find themselves still alive, were frisky and full of devilment. Their first thoughts were of the Padre.

"Hey, Padre," a voice would call out, carrying the length of the ward, "how's it hanging this morning?"

"Still dripping, Padre?"

"It's the hockey stick for you," another chimed in.

"Maybe your girlfriend will come to visit you. Then we can all have a go."

Humiliated beyond description, the Padre lay silently under his blankets, feigning sleep, as the raucous laughter and malicious taunts continued.

"Don't worry, Padre," a solicitous voice called out, "I've had three doses and I'm still going strong."

I laughed at this boast along with the others but was to find out later that day from an orderly that the statement was correct. Canadian soldiers had been overseas for four years, waiting to go into action. Some had gone to North Africa, some had fought at

Dieppe, and some fought in the invasions of Sicily and Italy, but the majority didn't get bloodied until the invasion of France. They proved themselves just as formidable in battle as when wreaking havoc in Britain for those four long years.

Constant training had bored them, and any opportunity to break the monotony was exploited to the full. Countless thousands were to marry British girls, who eventually came to Canada as war brides. The Canadian Army had literally taken over the British pubs and British girls – and British wives, in many cases. To say the army types were tough and rough is to understate what three and four years of constant army manoeuvres had done to their bodies. Sleeping in their uniforms on the ground in rainy England, continually on the march, they were in superb physical condition. The average daily route march was twenty-five miles, with full pack, carrying a nine pound rifle and wearing triple soled boots.

A lieutenant from the Essex Scottish Regiment had been brought to Watford after the fierce and bloody fighting at Caen, where the Canadians distinguished themselves. When he was sufficiently recovered from his bullet wounds, he wanted to get out of bed but found he couldn't walk. The soles of his feet had shed the two inch thick calluses that had built up over three years of marching, and they sloughed off his feet in layers. His feet were pink and tender as a baby's. Putting them on the floor made him yell with pain.

The ones who had been burned in their tanks were the hardest to live amongst. Ears, noses, hair, eyebrows, all gone. The nose, two tiny holes in a mass of scar tissue. The skin drawn tightly over the cheekbones and the mouth twisted and drawn up tight. Ears shrivelled into tiny corkscrews. Heads completely bald forever. I shrank from them for weeks, ashamed of my behaviour, but so deeply disturbed that I could not act or talk normally with them.

It was they who pushed the socializing. They would land on the end of my bed, clutching a deck of cards in a clawlike hand. "How about a game of knock rummy?" the twisted little mouth would say. Try as I would, it took weeks of close association before I was able to meet their eyes. Their courage and spirit, their complete lack of self pity, was overwhelming. Oh, the joy when they got their first hairpiece. Strutting around the ward with a hand mirror, they would pose and posture, slicking down an imaginary end with a wet finger.

"How about it? Don't I look great? How about that colour? No grey hair for me, chum. Wow, wait until the girls see me now."

They suffered countless operations under the expert surgeons who grafted skin from thighs, backs, and stomachs to build them noses and ears, and they endured all of it with great hope. I stood in complete awe of them. Except I couldn't stand. The doctor ordered me to stay in bed. I pleaded with him to release me since it was humiliating to feel fine and be surrounded by really sick people. "No," he said. "Not until your blood sedimentation stabilizes." Whatever that meant.

The English summer had finally arrived and our ward windows were wide open. Screenless, they afforded a great view of grass and trees. Through them we could watch the stream of orderlies, nurses, and doctors coming and going over the spacious grounds. We all wanted out of that hospital and the summer made it more appealing. We wanted out, even for a few hours. I don't know who suggested it, probably Vince, with his fertile mind, but someone said, "Why don't we all go down to the local pub tonight?" A stunned silence fell over the group of us who were playing cards.

"Great idea, but how do you suppose we could get out? They won't give us passes," said an army captain.

"Easy," Vince said, "we go out through the windows. Hell, they're big enough to drive a truck through."

The idea took hold and enthusiastic planning began. Clothes would have to be smuggled out of the large closets in the afternoon and hidden under the blankets. Wheelchairs could be folded and passed through the windows and the patient lifted through. No problem. The same with the crutches and canes. Those able to walk unassisted could push the wheelchairs.

"It's hardly a mile to the pub," Vince said, "we can make it easy."

"How about asking some of the orderlies to help?"

"No, for God's sake, they'll only get into shit if we get found out. Let's keep it to ourselves."

Excitement grew as the dinner trays were removed and the evening meal finished. Fortunately, the nursing station for our ward was around the corner and isolated. When the evening rounds had been made and the orderlies and nurses left the ward, we all got out of bed and started dressing. It took some careful manoeuvring to get several of the amputees through the window, but the wheelchairs were no problem and soon we started off, snorting with laughter and in high spirits. It felt so great to be free and headed for the first drink in many long weeks. Somehow we all made it safely down the winding English road to the pub.

How great to get inside a pub once more! The army types flung themselves into the beer and we had a party going and the piano banging in record time. The English patrons gave us the usual warm welcome and immediately a group challenged us to a dart game. Two guys in wheelchairs surprised even themselves by winning a game. The English girls must have spread the word for soon there were a dozen of them all praising the new toupees, so proudly exhibited. I marvelled at the complete lack of apprehension they showed to the newly grafted skin and mutilated faces of the Canadians. Their understanding was nothing short of sensational. They were sympathetic without being maudlin and exhibited complete empathy free of any pretence. Romances began blooming all over the pub as the affection-starved troops rose to the occasion.

When the pub owner called, "Time, Ladies and Gentlemen," we were all six sheets to the wind and having a wonderful time. "Aw, come on," we shouted, "one more round!" The publican was sympathetic to the cause. He, like his regular patrons, knew all about Watford hospital and how its patients had got there. But he was nervous.

"They'll cancel my licence. It's against the law to serve after hours."

"Just one round," we all chanted, "then you can close the bar."

After more persuasion he reluctantly said, "Well all right, but make it quick and mind, if the Bobbie shows up, we're all for it."

Cheers rang out and the fun continued, but we had really gone beyond our limit. Most of us had lost our holding capacity after our enforced absence. So slowly, after many farewells, we began the long trek home, still roaring with laughter and singing as we weaved and tottered up the road. The return journey is still a blur to me and like everyone else I fell asleep on top of the bed, fully dressed.

All of us missed breakfast the next morning, ignoring the nurses' demands to wake up. I didn't come fully awake until a cheer broke out and I roused myself to find a group gathered at a window, pointing and cheering. I joined them to see a weird sight. A straggling line of hospital orderlies was coming across the lawn pushing wheelchairs full of crutches and canes. Astonished, I finally realized that the wounded had all made it back on foot and the orderlies had been sent to collect the chairs and crutches.

A military hospital differs from a civilian hospital in many ways. As a civilian you can demand your release or change your doctor if you disagree with his treatment or even tell the doctor to get stuffed. Not so in a military hospital. You take orders and are under the same code of military discipline as on your regular unit. The CO of the hospital is the exalted ruler who has absolute disciplinary power over his patients. To disobey his orders is to be put on charge or arrested or even, if the case is serious enough, court martialled.

So usually, the staff is obeyed and order is maintained. But this was wartime. We weren't peacetime troops but civilians in uniform, and only for the duration of the war. So a lot of rules got badly bent and twisted, since no one cared a damn.

One evening a form was carried into our ward on a stretcher and put carefully in the bed opposite mine. The nurses and orderlies fluttered around, fussing over the man, all working in whispers. The Matron arrived to give the rest of us a few well chosen words.

"This man," she began, "has a very bad case of shell shock. It's imperative that he have complete quiet and rest. No sudden noises, no yelling or laughing or banging around. He must be kept quiet. Now I want all of you to promise to behave." She bustled out with her uniform rustling as we all stared at the bed and the unfortunate soldier.

Everything was quiet for a long time, everyone afraid to speak after the stern lecture from the Matron. *Crash*. We all jumped. A soldier had deliberately knocked his water jug off his night table. Instantly, the man in the bed leaped up screaming. "Help, help! Help me, we're being shelled! Oh God, help me, please!" His terrified screams scared the hell out of me and brought the nurses on the run and the ward alive with orderlies all trying to soothe the patient and get him back into bed. His screaming continued as they held him down and finally managed to calm him. I lay there petrified at the sight. "Now, now, it's all right. You're safe with us, nothing can hurt you." They spoke soothingly to him and he relaxed and lay back, moaning softly, his eyes closed.

Then the Matron arrived on the scene, firm of jaw, eyes blazing, her starched uniform rustling. She tore into all of us with a fierce and blistering attack on our detestable behaviour. She kept her voice low, but it fairly hissed with venom as she bit off each word. "You miserable, bloody bastards. I distinctly asked each and every one of you to behave. This man is sick, terribly sick. He must have complete rest and quiet. You made that noise deliberately to startle him. You should be absolutely ashamed of yourselves. You disgust me." Completely chastened we all lay there avoiding her eyes.

After she had flounced out, her heels clicking down the corridor, we all exchanged glances. Silent glances. A nurse came in to ask why the Matron was so angry and snapping at everyone. We told her it was all a misunderstanding. We settled back to read or work on our occupational therapy projects. Handmade leather gloves and wallets were the favourites. It helped pass the time and gave you a chance to play kneesy with the occupational therapist.

After half an hour had passed, the water jug smasher sat up in his bed and stared across the aisle at the shell shocked patient. "Hey, you!" he yelled. "Wake up, wake up! Get up man, we're under attack! Run man, run for your life!" and he began banging his bed pan on the iron railings of his bed. It was awful. The poor victim leaped screaming from his bed and ran, utterly out of control, careening from bed to bed, into the hall. His terrified screams echoed through the hospital as the entire lower floor erupted, people dashing everywhere.

How can anyone think such a thing funny? Yet we all roared with laughter. The patient never returned. He was placed in a private room far removed from his tormentor. Which probably should have been the wise first course.

But the Matron returned. Somehow she had figured out the guilty party and she marched directly to his bed. "Get out of that bed and come with me, now," she snapped. Meekly, the young officer obeyed. He, too, got a private room, but he had a military guard posted outside his door until the CO could decide on his punishment.

I was released from the hospital shortly after that episode to return to air force life. But I never forgot my army experience.

Over Home

There were now so many aircrew sitting around England that many were being shipped home to Canada. The powers that be said I should join them.

The Repatriation Depot was located at Warrington, near Liverpool, and I arrived with a buddy named Patterson late in October to await a troop ship. The CO was a guy named Massey – Denton Massey, it turned out, one of four Massey brothers from Toronto. Vincent Massey was the Canadian High Commissioner to London throughout the war; Raymond was in Hollywood making movies; and another brother, Hart, a Flight Lieutenant, served at RCAF Overseas Headquarters. I had seen Hart in London several times. Since he stood less than five feet it was impossible not to notice him. He looked like, and was often mistaken for, an air cadet. But this brilliant architect took it all in stride and was quite popular.

Denton was a different type. He had been a well known Bible teacher in Toronto before the war and was very devout. Quite a large man, he had the same build as my buddy Patterson. Warrington was full of regulations, especially galling after the more carefree squadron days. Every conceivable ruse was used to keep the airmen busy and out of jail. Church parade each Sunday was mandatory, and each was led by Denton Massey, who often read the Bible from the pulpit.

Unable to avoid it, I marched along to church on my first Sunday in camp. It proved worth the effort. Group Captain Denton Massey took a front pew and promptly fell asleep as the Padre droned along in his sermon. After a while, giant snores filled the church and all eyes turned to the front pew. There, in full and magnificent view, was Denton, snoring away and drowning out the Padre.

The next Sunday, Massey climbed to the pulpit to explain his previous behaviour and after apologizing he burst out crying. We all thought it was hilarious. I thought he might be an interesting man to meet but wasn't prepared when the opportunity arrived.

Our group was informed that we would soon get a ship to take us home and everyone began feverishly filling in the last nights in England by partying from pub to pub. Friend Patterson and I decided to go into Liverpool for one last visit and we made our plans over the bar. "I'll call a cab," I told him, "but make sure you're ready. They won't wait." I went out in the hall to use the phone, and then waited by the front door of the mess for the cab. It arrived in fast time and I told the driver we would be right out. I ran into the mess searching for Patterson. He was nowhere to be found. I searched the bar and the lounge but no Patterson. Fearful that the cab would leave I began a hurried search of the dining room. Still no Patterson. Where was that stupid bastard? Then suddenly in front of me was the unmistakable back of Patterson heading down a dim corridor.

Whack. I pounded my fist into his back between the shoulder blades, yelling, "You stupid son of a bitch, come on, the cab's waiting!"

Group Captain Denton Massey turned to face me. "Did you want me, Flying Officer?" I assured him I didn't and he gracefully accepted my blurted apologies.

Finally we were boarded on a ship that would take us home. Excited confusion was rampant as we explored the ship and found our quarters. As officers we were assigned to first class cabins, a far cry from the *Queen Elizabeth* and eighteen guys crammed into a tiny cabin. The food was magnificent and we settled in to enjoy the six day voyage, revelling in the comparative luxury.

On board were hundreds of English girls, some of the first war brides to sail for Canada. Each had married a Canadian serviceman and they were thrilled to be going to their new homes; even if their husbands were still fighting in France. They couldn't believe the quantity of food after four years of ration coupons and queuing for hours for a loaf of bread. Most had lost their taste for sugar and butter and refused to eat them. Many were worried about their future in a strange land and questioned all of us about Canada. None had any idea of the distances between cities, and many thought Toronto was the only major city. As we stood at the rail gazing over the empty ocean, one nervous bride asked me, "What's a squaw?" Baffled, I asked her why she wanted to know. "Well, I married a Canadian Indian, and some people say that makes me a squaw. What does it mean?"

Fighting for time to think up the best possible answer, I asked her where she was going. "I think it's south of Calgary." Then after a pause, "Is that near Toronto?" I went into some geography, still avoiding her question, but she persisted. "Am I a squaw?"

"Oh," I said, off-handedly, "that's just an old fashioned word. It's not used anymore. Don't worry about it." She seemed relieved and we parted, but it gave me a deeper appreciation of the trauma that faced many of these brave girls as they sailed towards their new and unknown world.

It wasn't until we could see lights on the shore that we realized we had reached the other side of the Atlantic. New York burst upon the horizon, a dazzling display of electricity that was frightening after years of blackouts. The Statue of Liberty torch was a shining beacon that we all recognized. I was home, safely home from the wars.

Epilogue

The last flight I made to Berlin is not recorded in my log book.

The very attractive German stewardess on the airliner carrying me to Berlin spoke excellent English. This, combined with the novelty of flying to Berlin in what happened to be a German aircraft, made the trip strangely thrilling.

It was 1961 and I was part of an RCAF hockey squad flying to Berlin for some exhibition games. The stewardess, it turned out, knew nothing about hockey but – and this was terribly important to me – she had grown up in Berlin and had lived there throughout the Battle of Berlin. I arranged to have dinner with her that evening.

I had been trying to get to Berlin ever since the war ended. I wanted to see the results of those bloody air battles. Now, eighteen years after the Battle of Berlin, it was finally happening, and my excitement and curiosity mounted as we broke through the clouds over Tempelhof aerodrome. Surely, there wouldn't be too much to see! We had destroyed over 600,000 buildings and killed over 200,000 Berliners. We had left it in flames, night after night, a maelstrom that could never survive as a city. I knew. I had seen it burning on eleven nights. I had seen the target photos taken after each raid: nothing but huge mounds of rubble and acre after acre of bombed out buildings. Over 50,000 tons of bombs had been dropped on the city by Bomber Command, and additional thousands by the American Eighth Air Force, not to mention the thirty-four tons from S Sugar. We had won the Battle of Berlin.

As our party gathered in the terminal building the first thing I requested from our hosts was a tour of the city. I didn't mention why.

It was an unbelievable tour. Beautiful buildings, gorgeous parks, modern steel and glass structures, picturesque bridges, wide tree-lined streets. Oh, here and there, an empty lot, grassed over. But rubble, destruction, bombed out buildings, roofless and windowless buildings, leaning skeletons of brick? No. We must have landed in the wrong city.

Completely confused I gaped as no other tourist has ever gaped. Nothing had happened here. There was no damage. Battle of Berlin? Obviously a fiction of youthful imagination. How could I ever have imagined this city in flames?

Hilda had been eight years old, she told me over dinner, during the Battle of Berlin. Now, at twenty-six, she too seemed to have difficulty remembering specifics. She had gone to school each day, climbing over the rubble which, after school, she had helped pile on the roadsides with her school friends. Most nights she had gone to the deep underground air raid shelters when our bombers came over. But she didn't elaborate on the bombings or the noise or the destruction, and seemed to accept it as normal. Food had been in desperately short supply and she could recall that the main part of any meal had been soup. But she could give me little of the horrors in detail. Her father, a government official, had evidently changed his lifestyle very little and she fascinated me with tales of how the average German father lived in pre-war and wartime Germany.

Her father had apparently never told her mother when he might be home for dinner, but he had insisted that the meal be placed on the table immediately he arrived home. There must be no waiting. If it was not served by the time he had taken his place at the table, he would get very angry and storm and shout at his wife. After dinner he would go to his bedroom, where he expected to find his clothes neatly laid out on the bed, his shoes newly shined, and his suit freshly pressed. He dressed and went off with his male friends to visit the beer gardens. His wife was never invited and the routine never varied. It was no different in other families. The man was the absolute head of the home and his wife was there to see to his every need.

Hilda claimed that the war didn't change her father's routine very much. It was only after the war ended that changes began. It started with the Americans who arrived as occupation troops. She could remember laughing with the other children, and sometimes with her parents, as they watched an American soldier pushing a baby carriage down the street. Her father thought it ridiculous for a man to do that, or anything else considered woman's work. He would not carry a parcel or shop for food. He would not wash a dish or help her mother around the house. But slowly that had all changed, and now you could see German fathers pushing baby carriages and running errands. "Even washing dishes," Hilda laughed.

I spent the next afternoon walking the streets of Berlin, dodging the sleek Mercedes Benz cars, trying to remember names and recall the faces of all my friends who had died over this city on those terrible winter nights of 1943.

For the moment I could not remember them. I could not recall the terror I had felt 20,000 feet above where I now stood. I could not visualize the horrible deaths my bombs had caused here. I had no feeling of guilt. I had no feeling of accomplishment.

As I stood looking skywards, it gradually dawned on me that I was recognizing that the war had finished long ago. If there was anything left here from those bomb filled nights, it had to be found, not in levelled buildings, but in the changed attitudes that Hilda had mentioned. I had been living in the past, while the Germans laughing and moving around me were determined to get on with the future.

It was the normal thing to do. Life went on – like it had for us in the war years, when, despite the destruction surrounding us, every new trip through the flak and the fighters was always going to be just another "piece of cake."